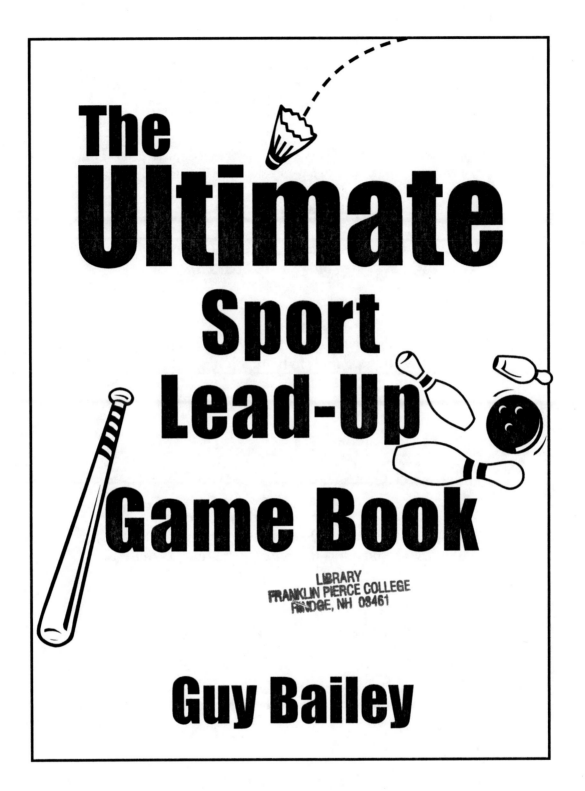

The Ultimate Sport Lead-Up Game Book

Guy Bailey

Educators Press

ISBN: 0-9669727-3 -2

Publisher's Cataloging-in-Publication
(Provided by Quality Books, Inc.)

Bailey, Guy, 1956-
    The ultimate sport lead-up game book: over 170 fun
& easy-to-use games to help you teach children
beginning sport skills/ Guy Bailey ; illustrated by
Cynthia Wilson, -- 3rd ed., Rev.
    p. cm.
    Includes index.
    LCCN: 00-191892
    ISBN: 0-9669727-3-2

    1. Physical education for children--Study and
teaching (Elementary)--Activity programs. 2. Sports for
children--Study and teaching (Elementary)--Activity
programs. 3. Games. I. Title.

GV443.B35 2001   372.86'044
                                  QBI00-762

The author and publisher assume that the reader will teach these games using professional judgement and
respect for student safety. In regards to this statement, the author and Educators Press shall have neither
liability nor responsibility in the case of injury to anyone participating in the activities contained within.

Educators Press

5333 NW Jackson St.
Camas, Wa. 98607
360-834-3049

Printed in the United States by:
Morris Publishing
3212 East Highway 30
Kearney, NE 68847
1-800-650-7888

I would like to dedicate this book to the students of Mill Plain Elementary School. They remind me everyday that the real joy of life is in its play.

NEVER FORGET THE KINDERGARTEN PRINCIPLE:

KEEP IT FUN !

A Word From The Author

If you were to reflect back to your favorite teachers, you would probably recognize a couple of things they all had in common: an undying enthusiasm for the subject matter they taught, and they made learning fun. We wanted to be there. Attending their class was the highlight of the school day. They produced an environment in which learning became play and play became learning. It is likely you developed a lasting enthusiasm for that particular subject matter because they made it meaningful to you.

As physical educators, it is my belief that our ultimate outcome should be to instill in our students an appreciation of and a *passion* for movement. As our favorite teachers did, we should desire to have students who literally can't wait to get to school every morning because... "Today is P.E.!" What's the best way of achieving a high and lasting level of student enthusiasm? Simple. Keep it fun! Robert Fulghum's advice in his book *All I Really Need To Know I Learned In Kindergarten* is true for kindergartners and it's true for adults.

Even though we're competing against the television set, computer games, video movies, and a myriad of other modern day attractions for kids, we can and we *must* make game playing, sports, dance, and exercise a more attractive alternative. We can start by choosing learning activities for our students that are meaningful to them. Make it fun! It's the fuel that provides the long-term motivation to live an active, healthy lifestyle now and later as adults.

My desire is that this book will assist you in your quest to make physical education the highlight of your students' day. For your students, I hope it launches a lifetime of moving, learning, and fun — that they continue playing beyond the walls of your gymnasium, motivated forever because of what happened inside those gym walls.

"Sports is the toy department of human life."

- Howard Cosell

ACKNOWLEDGMENTS

Special thanks to my wife, Shelby, for her constant encouragement and patience during the entire production of this book. Her daily support and love are gifts I treasure the most in life.

I am also grateful for the understanding and support of my two sons, Justin and Austin. They were my "first students," and I have learned so very much about teaching, children, and life, through my role as their father.

I would also like to acknowledge Cynthia Wilson for her outstanding illustrations and valued assistance in making this book a reality. As with my other book, *The Ultimate Playground & Recess Game Book,* Cynthia's illustrations help tremendously in the visual understanding of each game's setup and play procedures.

A special "thanks" goes out to my colleagues at Mill Plain Elementary School in Vancouver, Washington. Your caring attitude and professionalism have contributed to making this special school a nuturing, safe, and fun place for children— and for adults!

I wish to also acknowledge the professionals at Morris Publishing, the company that did the printing and cover design for this book. From the very first phone call to the finished product, the professionals there were an absolute delight to work with.

CONTENTS

A Word From The Author   5
Preface   11
The Role of Sport Lead-Up Games   15

Chapter One   Football   19

Progression Guide   20   Kick-Off Attack   32
No-Ball Football   21   Capture The Footballs   33
Sack The Quarterback   22   Football 100   34
Bamboozle'em Football   23   End Zone   35
Punt and Pass Relay   24   49'er Football   36
Five Catches   25   Fake 'Em' Out   37
Hike 'N' Catch   26   Boom It Over   38
Knock 'Em' Down   27   Field Goal Contest   39
Punt Attack   28   Aerobic Football Kicking 40
Battle Ball   29   Four Downs   41
Hike & Pass   30   One Chance Football   42
Home Run Football   31   Flicker Football   43
                                     Run 'N' Gun   44

Chapter Two   Soccer   45

Progression Guide   46   3-On-3 Mini-Soccer   58
Mass Soccer   47   Line Soccer   59
Soccer Red Light -Green Light 48   Sideline Soccer   60
Crab Soccer   49   Heading Relay Races   61
Soccer Maniacs   50   Backstop Soccer   62
Soccer Tunnel Tag   51   Scores Galore   63
The Soccer Bull   52   Four Ball Shootout   64
Dribble Freeze Tag   53   Soccer Croquet   65
Soccer Pirates   54   Rotation Soccer   66
Pin-Ball Soccer   55   Four Team Soccer   67
Circle Soccer   56   Modified Soccer   68
Soccer Steal The Bacon   57

Chapter Three   Lacrosse   69

Progression Guide   70   Possession   77
Throw & Go   71   End Zone Lacrosse   78
Circle Pepper   72   Scoop 'Crosse   79
Pass Relay   73   Lacrosse Tennis   80
Fly Back   74   Crosse Softball   81
Keep Away   75   Sideline Lacrosse   82
Diamond Run-A-Round   76   Royal Lacrosse   83

Chapter Four

		Basketball	85
Progression Guide	86	Five Passes	96
No Rules Basketball	87	Pass Ball	97
Basketball Pirates	88	Basketball Golf	98
Gotcha!	89	End Zone Basketball	99
Bull In The Ring	90	Knock Out	100
King of the Dribblers	91	Half-Court Basketball	101
H-O-R-S-E	92	Three-On-Three	102
Around The World	93	Triple Play	103
Twenty-One	94	Basket Bordenball	104
Runners & Gunners	95	Sideline Basketball	106

Chapter Five

		Hockey	107
Progression Guide	108	Ground Attack	116
Hockey Pirates	109	Shooting Goals	117
Circle Race	110	Lotsa Pucks	118
Hockey Steal	111	Goalies Galore	119
Pyramid Passing	112	3-On-3 Hockey	120
Run 'n' Weave	113	Sideline Hockey	121
Hockey Keep Away	114	Position Hockey	122
Line Hockey	115	Modified Hockey	123

Chapter Six

		Volleyball	125
Progression Guide	126	Air Raid	133
Catch 22	127	Serve 'Em' Over	134
Newcomb	128	Points Galore	135
Keep It Up	129	Big Ball Volleyball	136
No Rules Volleyball	130	Hit The Board	137
V-O-L-L-E-Y	131	Sideline Volleyball	138
A-B-C Relay	132	Three & Over	139
		Four-Square Volleyball	140

Chapter Seven

		Badminton	141
Progression Guide	142	No Net Badminton	146
Birdie Relay	143	Shuttle 'Minton	147
Flying Birdies	144	Volleyminton	148
Badminton Keep-It-Up	145	Mass Badminton	149

Chapter Eight

		Tennis	151
Progression Chart	152	Floor Ping Pong	157
Tennis Dribble Relay	153	No Racket Tennis	158
Clean The Court	154	Tennis Keep Away	159
Tennis Knockout	155	Horse Tennis	160
No Rules Tennis	156	Tennis 'Round The World	161
		Pickleball	162

Chapter Nine   Track & Field   163

Progression Guide	164	Pony Express	168
Stretch Tag	165	Team Cross Country	169
Loose 'n' Limber Tag	166	Hula Hoop Long Jumping	170
Sprint Tag	167	Hula Hoop Discus Throw	171
		Modified Shot Put	172
		Team Olympics	173

Chapter Ten   Softball   179

Progression Guide	180	Slugger Ball	190
Baserunning Relay	181	Throw & Run Softball	191
Around The Horn	182	One Chance Softball	192
Hot Taters	183	Add 'Em Up	193
Grounder Ball	184	Long Base	194
In A Pickle	185	No-Team Softball	195
Kickball	186	Home Run	196
Throw & Go	187	No-Outs Softball	197
Tee-Ball	188	Three-Team Softball	198
No-Outs Kickball	189	Modified Slo-Pitch	199
		Mat Kickball	200

Chapter Eleven   Golf   201

Progression Guide	202	Frisbee Golf	205
Beanbag Golf	203	Croquet Golf	206
Soccer Golf	204	Mini Golf	207

Chapter Twelve   Bowling   209

Progression Guide	210	Soccer Bowling	213
Beanbag Bowling	211	Frisbee Bowling	214
Aerobic Bowling	212		

Chapter Thirteen   Miscellaneous Sports   215

Progression Guide	216	Cricketball	221
Beanbag Horseshoes	217	No Tackle Rugby	222
Modified Bocce	218	One Chance Rugby	223
Bocce Croquet	219	Deck Tennis	224
Croquet Billards	220	Outside Billards	225
		Mini-Team Handball	226

Index   229

A teacher affects eternity; he can never tell where his influence stops.

Henry Brooks Adams

Preface

During the course of my 20 years as a physical educator, I have constantly been on the hunt for challenging and exciting sport lead-up games. In my search I discovered that many of the games did offer some skill learning but were absent of fun and meaning. These elements are so critical for long-term student enjoyment and motivation. Likewise, some of the lead-up games created some level of student excitement but were sorely lacking in skill development. I couldn't justify the inclusion of these games into my curriculum.

After coming up empty-handed in my search for that one sport lead-up game book that met my student needs, I decided to take matters into my own hands. Thus, *The Ultimate Sport Lead-Up Game Book* was given birth. Finally, a single all-inclusive resource of the very best skill-building games for more than 12 different sports is now available for everyone! These games are both skill-based *and* fun-packed. My students have benefited tremendously from the use of these games and I'm certain that they'll become powerful learning experiences for your students too.

Lead-up games for basketball, football, hockey, track & field, volleyball, lacrosse, soccer, badminton, tennis, softball, golf, and bowling were selected because they are a prominent part of the K-12 curriculum and after-school sport offerings available to our youth. Elementary and middle school physical education curriculums usually focus on "leading up" games because of the developmental needs of this age group. Please keep in mind that this book is not intended to be a complete physical education curriculum for any grade level. Its purpose is to supplement your sport skill units in both the elementary and middle school curriculums. Specific sport and fundamental skills are not analyzed in this book since that information is readily available elsewhere. The book's emphasis is on providing you with a unique resource of sport lead-up games in which sport skills and game strategies can be practiced in a fun and meaningful setting.

Each lead-up game is described and illustrated in a clear and easy-to-understand format. The developmentally appropriate arrangement will also make it simple and quick to find games that will meet your needs and lessen your preparation time. Another unique feature of this book is the section devoted to explaining the importance of sport lead-up games as part of a balanced curriculum. Both the beginning and experienced teacher will find invaluable information about the educational benefits of lead-up games, along with game selection and student safety tips.

-Preface continued on next page

The Ultimate Sport Lead-Up Game Book will appeal not only to those who teach physical education but also to many professionals outside the school setting. Youth coaches, camp directors and community recreational leaders will discover skill-building games that are exciting, fun, meaningful, and adaptable to their own particular situations.

It is my personal belief that the ultimate goal of physical educators is to have our students leave the gym full of excitement and motivation for learning, and carrying that on to areas of their lives that go beyond the physical education experience. We owe it to them to provide success-oriented learning experiences that leave them craving for more. These games have done that with my students. It's my sincere hope and desire that your students, too, will leave your PE class excited and asking...

"Can we please do that again?!"

In teaching, the greatest sin is to be boring.

J.F. Herbart

The Role Of
Sport Lead-up Games

Sports are so much a part of the average American child's lifestyle that little justification is needed for including sport-related activities in our physical education curriculums. Children as young as kindergarten age are playing in recreational leagues that feature soccer, basketball, and baseball (or tee-ball). There is an ever-growing number of kids playing organized hockey and youth football. In most areas, you'll see elementary track & field programs as well. Additionally, many elementary schools now offer after-school intramurals involving sports such as volleyball, floor hockey, gymnastics and indoor soccer. These sport activities give our children valuable opportunities for physical, emotional, and social growth and have long been a part of our physical education programs.

A Definition of a "Lead-up" Game

A lead-up game can be categorized as a modified game utilizing one or more of the fundamental skills, rules, and strategies of a particular sport. These modified games often start with simple activities involving a few skills for the younger and/or less-skilled student. Eventually more challenging activities involving several skill tasks are introduced. The "leading-up" approach, using modified games, allows students to develop sport skills sooner with greater interest and meaning. This developmentally-based approach to skill learning has long been an established and effective teaching technique. In fact, the approach of using "lead-up" activities can also be applied to developing student skills outside the domain of team and recreational sports (recess games, gymnastics, dance, etc.)

The Value of Lead-up Games

As any physical educator or youth coach will tell you, the "game" is what children really look forward to. They don't want to practice endlessly one specific skill; they would much rather "get on to the game." Formal drills, for an extended amount of time, require a lot of self-discipline and few students are sufficiently motivated to do that. Most students will want to learn as they play. A high level of student interest will be maintained if skills can be practiced through the use of fun and challenging lead-up games. As previously mentioned, student enthusiasm and motivation is so important to learning.

The use of lead-up games should not diminish the necessity and importance of drills. Teacher instruction, drills, and lead-up games still provide the optimal learning experience. Drills and student practice perhaps need to be emphasized as "leading up to the game" type of activities. Keep in mind, that it's not uncommon to have students develop a more intense interest in practicing their skills once they have participated in lead-up games. They understand better how a particular skill fits into a game situation.

Another value of lead-up games is the opportunity for educators to choose learning experiences that are appropriate for his or her specific class needs. The less skilled can play a less difficult game. Likewise, the more highly gifted can play a more complex game. Skill level differences can be managed by having simultaneous groups play lead-up games of various levels of difficulty and complexity. In fact, one of the greatest challenges facing physical educators today is to have a program that is flexible and adaptable to all students. Lead-up games can help you meet that challenge.

Maximum student participation is another desired goal for most physical educators. For those of you with large classes, this can be a problem. Additionally, regulation sports are not always conducive to having a large number of players participating at one time. Unless you have multiple courts, basketball is a good example of a limited participatory activity. Fortunately, there are basketball lead-up games that will allow you to use many more players than the regulation game.

Another value of lead-up sports is positive competition. Competition has been given a bad rap in recent years among some physical educators and, at times, justifiably so. Unfortunately, we've all witnessed educators and coaches that have focused entirely too much on the winning aspect of playing a game. Competition should not be to "prove" but rather to "improve." Competition can bring out the best in a person when it is correctly approached. The teaching style of an educator, more so than the game itself, is often the deciding factor in whether competition is a positive student experience or not. Since competition is inherent in our lives and in our society, lead-up games can provide valuable "leading-up" lessons in learning how to handle the competitive times we will all face in life.

In summary, lead-up sport games offer students a unique and valuable learning experience. The many benefits they offer to our students and to our programs make it a necessity to include those sport lead-up games that are developmentally appropriate into our physical education programs.

Questions To Ask When Selecting A Lead-Up Game

Here are a few suggested questions an educator might want to ask in evaluating and selecting sport lead-up games.

• Will the game(s) meet a specific learning objective? There are many lead-up games that can help you not only reach fundamental skill objectives, but social and emotional objectives as well.

• Have the required skills for this game been previously taught so that the students can experience success? The teacher's instruction of a skill(s) should always come before game situations.

• Is this a developmentally appropriate game for my class? Your students' physical and mental maturity levels will dictate the type of game you should use. Select games that are challenging but not overly difficult.

• Does this game allow for maximum student participation? If not, consider modifying a game to fit your own particular needs. For example, if you have a large class, consider playing two games simultaneously (provided you have ample space).

Safety Guidelines For Using Lead-up Games

The following guidelines will help reduce the possibility of accidents happening during class. Although the lead-up games in this book are quite safe, the teacher still needs to use professional judgment when presenting any type of learning experience to his or her students.

✔ Teach and model safe behaviors. Emphasize safety practices, precautions, and rules with each class and each new game.
✔ Provide an adequate warm-up prior to game participation.
✔ Make sure the playing areas have ample room. Stay away from fences, walls, poles, and other obstacles.
✔ Clear playing area of any debris and hazardous objects. Require all students to wear athletic shoes.
✔ Closely supervise all students at all times. Carefully monitor and enforce all guidelines.

* Please note that the term he and him are used throughout this book to represent both genders equally.

CHAPTER ONE

FOOTBALL

FOOTBALL GAME PROGRESSION GUIDE

GAME	GRADE LEVELS			
	K-2	3-4	5-6	7-8
No-Ball Football	X	X		
Sack The Quarterback	X	X		
Bamboozle 'Em Football	X	X		
Punt and Pass Relay		X	X	
Five Catches		X	X	
Hike 'N' Catch		X	X	
Knock 'Em Down		X	X	
Punt Attack		X	X	
Battle Ball		X	X	
Hike & Pass		X	X	
Home Run Football		X	X	
Kick-Off Attack		X	X	
Capture The Footballs		X	X	
Football 100		X	X	X
End Zone		X	X	X
49'er Football		X	X	X
Fake 'Em Out			X	X	X
Boom It Over		X	X	X
Field Goal Contest		X	X	X
Aerobic Football Kicking		X	X	X
Four Downs		X	X	X
One Chance Football		X	X	X
Flicker Football			X	X
Run 'N' Gun			X	X

NO-BALL FOOTBALL

SKILL OBJECTIVES: Running; dodging; flag pulling

EQUIMENT: Flags for each player; cone markers

GAME SETUP: Use the floor markings for boundaries if playing in the gymnasium. For outside play, set up a rectangular size field with the cone markers. Divide the class into two teams. Assign offensive and defensive teams with each team standing on opposite goal lines facing each other.

HOW TO PLAY: *No-Ball Football* introduces the younger students to the chasing and fleeing concept in football, as well the terminology used in football such as "offense" and "defense."

On a starting signal, the offensive players attempt to run through the defensive players to the opposite goal line. Once past the goal line, the offensive players are safe and can stop running. The defensive players chase the offensive players, attempting to pull as many flags as possible. Tally up the number of flags pulled after each play. Reverse the roles and continue playing.

SCORING: Challenge the students to pull as many flags possible and/or to make it safely to the opponents' goal line when on offense. If keeping score, the team that pulls the most flags at the conclusion of play wins the game.

SACK THE QUARTERBACK

SKILL OBJECTIVES: Pulling flags; chasing and fleeing

EQUIPMENT: Two flags for each player

GAME SETUP: All players are to wear two flags (hanging from a belt or back pockets). Select two players (the "sackers") to stand inside a center circle. The other players (the "quarterbacks") start by standing outside the circle.

HOW TO PLAY: This chasing and fleeing game introduces the concept of pulling flags for the primary grade level student. Flag pulling is an important element to the more advanced lead-up games to football which are described in this book.

  The game begins with the quarterbacks slowly edging closer and closer to the sackers. At any time the sackers can yell out "sack!" When this happens, the sackers chase the quarterbacks, attempting to pull their flags before they make across one of the four safety boundary lines. Once a quarterback crosses a boundary line he is safe. If a quarterback has his flag pulled, he becomes a sacker and joins them each time in the center circle.

SCORING: There is no scoring. The objective is to be the last quarterback remaining before the game ends.

BAMBOOZLE 'EM FOOTBALL

SKILL OBJECTIVES: Running, dodging; pulling flags; huddling; stance position

EQUIPMENT: Flags for each player; cones markers; a coin

GAME SETUP: For outside play, use the cone markers to make a rectangular shaped playing area. For inside play, use the floor markings of a basketball court. Divide the class into two equal teams with each team standing on opposite goal lines facing each other. All players are to wear flags.

HOW TO PLAY: This game is a natural continuation of the previous game (*No-Ball Football*). The skills of chasing and flag pulling are now combined with the new concepts of huddling, getting into a 3-point stance position, starting signals, scoring a "touchdown," and so on.

Start with the offensive team forming a huddle around the game leader. The game leader gives a coin to one of the players (without letting the defensive team see which player received it). Before breaking the huddle, the game leader should ask all the offensive players to close both fists so that the defensive doesn't know has the "football." Both teams are to then assume a 3-point stance on their goal lines.

When the game leader calls out "ready, set, hike," the offensive players run toward the opposite goal line, with the defensive players running forward and attempting to pull their flags. Upon having his flag pulled, the offensive player is top running and reveal whether or not he has the coin. A touchdown is scored if the player with the coin successfully crosses the goal line without having his flag pulled. After each play, have the teams reverse roles and continue playing.

SCORING: The player with the coin scores a touchdown when he makes it to the goal line without having a flag pulled. A touchdown is worth 6 points.

PUNT & PASS RELAY

SKILL OBJECTIVES: Punting, passing, kicking

EQUIPMENT: One football for each player

GAME SETUP: Have each player stand on a goal line with a football in his possession. The players need to be spaced at least 10-15 feet apart.

HOW TO PLAY: The objective is to be the first player to cross the opposite goal line (usually 100 yards away), or to reach the goal line in the fewest pass and punt attempts.
   On a signal, each player begins by punting the ball down the field as far as possible. He then moves up to the spot where his ball has stopped. On the next signal, each player passes the ball as far as possible, and then moves up to that spot. Play continues in this fashion until all the players have successfully crossed the goal line.

SCORING: Challenge each student to a lower score (that is, the fewest number of pass and punt attempts to reach the goal line) each time they play. If keeping score, the first player that crosses the opposite goal line wins the contest.

TEACHING SUGGESTIONS: To have the game last longer, consider having the students cross the opposite goal line and then work back toward the beginning goal line.
   For safety purposes, make sure the students maintain adequate spacing throughout the playing of the game.

FIVE CATCHES

SKILL OBJECTIVES: Throwing; catching; running; guarding

EQUIPMENT: One football per game; pinnies for each team; cones if playing outdoors

GAME SETUP: This game can be played either in a gymnasium or outside. Form two teams of 5-7 players. For larger classes, play multiple games if space permits.

HOW TO PLAY: The objective is for a team to make five consecutive passes to five different players without dropping the ball or having it intercepted. To begin, have all players scatter throughout the playing area. Each player is assigned to guard one player on the opposing team. No "double-teaming" is allowed. No personal contact is allowed. When a player has the ball, he can not take more than three steps. Nor can the player hold the ball for more than three seconds. The ball will be rewarded to the opposing team if the above violations occur.

SCORING: The first team to make five successful catches either wins the game or scores a point.

HIKE 'N' CATCH

SKILL OBJECTIVES: Hiking; catching

EQUIPMENT: One football per team

GAME SETUP: Form teams of 4-6 players. Have the teams line up in a straight line with each player spaced about 3-5 yards apart. The first player in each team should have a football.

HOW TO PLAY: The game objective is to be the first team to finish hiking the ball. The game begins with the first player in each team hiking the ball to the player who is directly behind him. If the ball touches the ground because of a fumble or bad hike, it is returned to the center who must hike it again. If caught, the player catching the ball hikes it to the next, and so on. When the last player gets the ball, he runs to the front of the team and starts hiking again. Play continues until a team is back in its original position.

SCORING: Challenge each team to finish as quickly as possible. If keeping score, award one point to the team that returns first to its original starting position.

KNOCK 'EM DOWN

SKILL OBJECTIVES: Throwing for accuracy; catching

EQUIPMENT: Foam footballs; 10 -14 bowling pins; cone markers if outside

GAME SETUP: This game can be played either outside or inside. If outside, use cone markers to set up a rectangular shaped field with a dividing line down the middle. If inside, use the floor markings of the basketball court. Space bowling pins several feet apart behind each team's back line. Divide the class into two equal teams. Each team starts with two footballs.

HOW TO PLAY: The game objective is to knock down as many of the opponents' bowling pins as possible. All players need to be instructed to stay on their half of the playing area. Players can throw the balls at the pins from anywhere behind the center dividing line. Players can intercept or knock down any pass attempts at the pins. Add more footballs throughout the game.

SCORING: A team has won the contest if they have either knocked down all of their opponents' pins, or if they have knocked over a higher number of pins in a designated time period.

TEACHING SUGGESTION: For safety reasons, it is highly recommended that only foam footballs be used in this game. Plastic, lightweight bowling pins are going to be easier to knock down (as opposed to regular bowling pins) when using the foam footballs.

PUNT ATTACK

SKILL OBJECTIVES: Punting; catching; running; dodging

EQUIPMENT: Flags for each player; enough footballs for half of the class; cone markers

GAME SETUP: Mark off a field about half the size of a regulation football field. Divide the class up into two equal teams. Assign one team to punt first, with each player holding a football on a goal line. The other team is to scatter on their half of the field. Playing multiple games on different fields will result in smaller team sizes.

HOW TO PLAY: The game objective is for a receiving player to catch a punt and return the ball across the opponent's goal line without having his flag pulled. On a starting signal, each member of the punting team is to punt his football as far as possible. The receiving players attempt to catch the punted balls, run through the punters (who are now trying to pull flags), and score touchdowns by crossing the goal line. Receivers are to stop running if their flags are pulled. Have the teams reverse roles and continue playing. Tally up the number of "touchdowns" after each play.

SCORING: A player is awarded one point (a "touchdown") for successfully carrying a football across the opponents' goal line without losing a flag.

BATTLE BALL

SKILL OBJECTIVES: Throwing; catching

EQUIPMENT: Foam footballs; volleyball net

GAME SETUP: Use a volleyball court or similar shaped playing area. Divide the class into two equal teams. If space permits, try playing multiple games simultaneously to allow for smaller team sizes.

HOW TO PLAY: The objective is to throw the footballs over the net as quickly as possible so that more will end up on the opponents' side when time has expired. Start with each player holding a foam football. On a signal, they begin passing and retrieving footballs. Play 1-3 minute "quarters" and at the end of each quarter, count the number of footballs on each side. Four quarters completes the game.

SCORING: Challenge each team to have the fewest number of footballs on its court after each quarter. If keeping score, the team with the fewest footballs is awarded one point.

TEACHING SUGGESTION: For safety purposes, it is strongly recommended that only foam footballs be used.

An alternative to throwing the footballs over the net would be to have the players punt, or to use any combination of punting and passing to get the balls over the net.

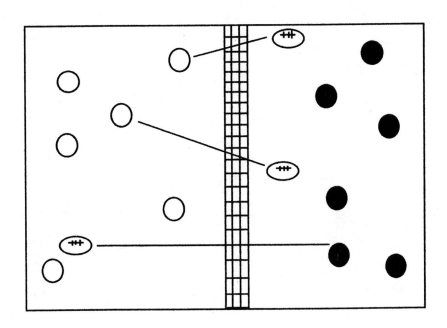

HIKE & PASS

SKILL OBJECTIVES: Hiking; passing; catching; stance position

EQUIPMENT: One football per group of three players

GAME SETUP: Three players to a team; form multiple teams.

HOW TO PLAY: The groups start on a starting goal line, facing the opposite goal line. Check each group for proper positioning. One player begins as the quarterback, another as the center, and the third player is the pass receiver. The pass receiver is to line up in a 3-point stance next to the center.

On a command, each quarterback calls out "ready, set, hike!" The ball is then hiked to the quarterback and passed to the receiver (who has run downfield after the "hike" command). If caught, the ball is placed on the ground at that spot. Receivers are not to continue running after the reception. As quickly as possible, the players rotate positions and stand ready for the next play. If the pass was incomplete, the team rotates positions and will play the next down from their original spot.

The rotation of players is as follows: The quarterback moves to pass receiver; the receiver to center; and the center becomes the quarterback.

SCORING: Challenge your students to complete as many passes possible. If keeping score, the first team to reach the opposite goal line wins the contest.

TEACHING SUGGESTION: Consider having your students play for an indefinite amount of time, going back and forth between goal lines. Challenge them to score as many "touchdowns" as possible.

QUARTERBACK   CENTER   RECEIVER

HOME RUN FOOTBALL

SKILL OBJECTIVES: Throwing; punting; kicking; catching; running

EQUIPMENT: One football; four bases, and one kicking tee for each game

GAME SETUP: The game is played using a softball field. Divide the class into groups of 7-10 players. For larger classes, set up multiple playing areas. Players are to number off, with player #1 standing at home base with the football. The other players are to scatter throughout the playing area.

HOW TO PLAY: The game begins with player #1 (standing at home base with the football) either passing, punting, or kicking the football out into the field. He then runs the bases just as a player would do if playing softball. The players in the field quickly retrieve the football and either throw or run the ball to home base. At that time, the baserunner stops. The baserunner is awarded one point for each base touched before the ball reached home base. After each play, the baserunner goes to the field and the player with the next number goes to home base (to have his chance at scoring). This rotation continues throughout the game.

SCORING: Baserunners are awarded one point for each base touched before having to stop. Challenge the players to score as many points possible.

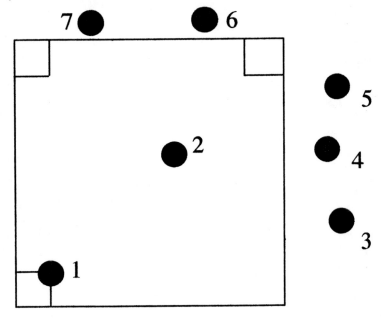

KICK-OFF ATTACK

SKILL OBJECTIVES: Kicking; catching; dodging; running

EQUIPMENT: Flags for each player; cone markers; enough footballs and kicking tees for half of the class.

GAME SETUP: Mark off a playing area that is about half the size of a regular football field. Divide the class into two equal teams. Assign one team to kick first from their goal line. The players on the receiving team stand near the opposite goal line.

HOW TO PLAY: The kicking team starts with their footballs placed on tees. On a signal, they run forward and kick the footballs as far as possible toward their opponents. Each member of the receiving team attempts to catch a kicked ball, run past the kickers (who are now trying to pull their flags), and make it to the opposite goal line without having his flag pulled. Those receivers who have their flags pulled can not continue running. Count the number of players who successfully crossed the goal line after each play. The teams reverse roles and play again.

SCORING: Six points (or a "touchdown") is awarded to each player that successfully carries a football across the goal line without losing a flag.

CAPTURE THE FOOTBALLS

SKILL OBJECTIVES: Throwing; catching; running; dodging

EQUIPMENT: Four footballs; flags for each player; cone markers; two large hula hoops; jump ropes

GAME SETUP: This game can be played outdoors or in the gymnasium. For indoor play, use the basketball court markings as boundaries. For outside play, use the cones to mark off a rectangular-shaped playing area. A center line divides the playing area into two halves. Place a hula hoop, with two footballs inside each hoop, by both of the end lines. Using ropes or tape, mark off two corner areas to be used as prisons.

Divide the class into two equal teams. Each player wears a flag set and stands on his designated end line to start the game.

HOW TO PLAY: The objective is for one team to capture the opponents' two footballs, along with keeping its own two balls. Once a team has all four footballs inside its hula hoop, the game is either finished or a score has occured.

The game begins with each team lined up near the center dividing line. On a signal, some of the players cross the center line attempting to capture the footballs while the others stay back and defend. Try to discourage a team from having more than one or two players guarding the balls and the prison. The ball may be advanced by either running with it or passing to a teammate. A ball that is dropped must be returned to the ball hula hoop.

A player must go to prison if his flag is pulled while on the opponents' side. If he had a football at the time his flag was pulled, he would have to put it back inside the hula hoop before going to prison. Prisoners can be freed only if one of their own players successfully makes it into the prison without having his own flag pulled. When freed, a prisoner must hold the hand of the player freeing him; they have to walk back to their own side before attempting to play again.

SCORING: Challenge each team to capture the opponents' two footballs, and to prevent their two footballs from being stolen. Play ends when one team has all four footballs inside its hula hoop.

TEAM 1 - ○
TEAM 2 - ●

FOOTBALL 100

SKILL OBJECTIVES: Passing, catching, hiking, pass defense

EQUIPMENT: One football per group of four students

GAME SETUP: Divide the class into groups of four students each. Each of the players assume a starting position as either the quarterback, center, receiver, or pass defender. The receiver is to line up next to the center in a three point stance. The pass defender lines up facing the receiver. This game is best played outside because of the space required.

HOW TO PLAY: The object of the game is to be the first player to score 100 points.

The play begins with the quarterback yelling out "ready, set, hike." The center then hikes the ball to the quarterback and the receiver runs downfield for a pass. The pass defender attempts to stay as close as possible to the receiver trying to prevent a pass completion. The receiver is awarded 10 points if he successfully catches the pass. However, if the pass defender intercepts the pass, he is awarded 10 points instead. An incomplete pass is not worth any points.

Players are to rotate positions after each play. The quarterback moves to receiver, the receiver moves to pass defender, the pass defender goes to center, and the center becomes the next quarterback.

SCORING: The first player to collectively score 100 points can be declared the winner.

TEACHING SUGGESTION: It is suggested that you teach proper pass defending techniques before the introduction of this game. Students need to know that improper touching or pushing of the receiver (or of the pass defender by the receiver) results in a "pass interference" penalty. If this happens, the player that was illegally touched or pushed is awarded 10 points.

RECEIVER   PASS DEFENDER

○   ●

○   ○

QUARTERBACK   CENTER

END ZONE

SKILL OBJECTIVES: Throwing; catching

EQUIPMENT: 2-10 foam footballs; cone markers

GAME SETUP: With the cone markers, mark off a playing area as shown below. The game can be successfully played in the gym or outdoors.

The students are divided into two equal teams. Half of each team starts the game standing in a designated end zone area. Begin the game with one football.

HOW TO PLAY: The objective is to throw a ball into the end zone and have it caught by a teammate. Players are to throw the football past and over the opposing players. A player can run up to the center line to throw a football or to block an opponent's pass, but cannot cross it. Likewise, players can not cross the end zone lines. A successful catch by an end zone player counts as a point. Footballs that go into an end zone are thrown back to teammates. However, only catches made by the end zone players count as points.

Each team is to have its players rotate positions halfway through the contest. Add more footballs throughout the playing of the game.

SCORING: A catch by an end zone player counts as one point. Catches by the non-end zone players do not count as points.

TEACHING SUGGESTION: This game involves the use of multiple footballs being thrown back and forth. For safety purposes, only foam footballs should be used.

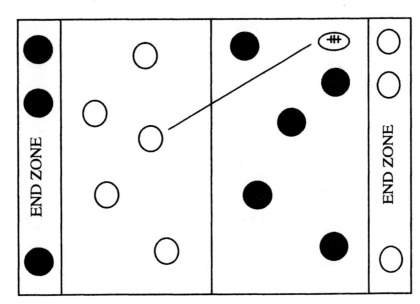

TEAM 1 - O
TEAM 2 - ●

49'ER FOOTBALL

SKILL OBJECTIVES: Passing, hiking, catching, pass defense

EQUIPMENT: One football for each game; cones, pinnies

GAME SETUP: Divide the class into teams of four students each. The offensive team consists of a quarterback, center, and two pass receivers. The defensive team consists of three pass defenders and one pass rusher. Mark off a playing area as shown in the illustration below.

HOW TO PLAY: The game objective is to be the first team to score exactly 49 points. Points are scored each time a pass is completed, with the point value dependent upon where the receiver caught the pass. An incomplete pass is not worth any points.

The offensive team starts with a center hike to the quarterback. The pass receivers, including the center, run out in the various scoring areas. The quarterback can pass to any of the receivers. The defensive pass rusher must count outloud to ten before he can cross the line of scrimmage attempting to tag the quarterback. The play automatically ends if the quarterback is tagged before getting the pass off.

The teams switch places after each play. Players should rotate positions each time they are on offense so that each team member has a chance to play quarterback, center, and receiver.

SCORING: If keeping score, the first team to reach exactly 49 points wins the game.

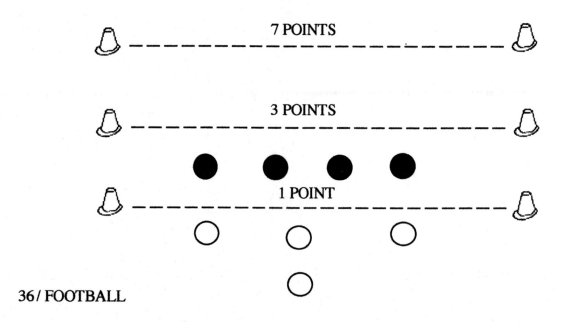

FAKE 'EM OUT

SKILL OBJECTIVES: Throwing; catching; running; defensive play

EQUIPMENT: 2-10 footballs; pinnies for each team; cone markers

GAME SETUP: With the cones, mark off playing area boundaries. An area about 3-5 yards wide, known as the "No-Man's Area," needs to exist in the middle of the playing area. Students are divided into two teams, with each team having half of its members on each side of the No-Man's Area. Both teams start with one football.

HOW TO PLAY: This is a great activity to help students understand the necessity for movement in football either in faking a defensive player to get open for a pass, or in guarding an offensive player so he can't receive a pass.

    The objective is to complete a pass to a teammate on the other side of the No-Man's Area. Players can run with the football anywhere on their side of the field, however, they can not cross the No-Man's Area. No touching or rough play is allowed. Add more and more footballs throughout the game.

SCORING: Each team is awarded one point for a completed pass. The teams can tally up their point totals at the completion of each "quarter" or designated time period. Challenge the teams to achieve higher point totals each quarter.

TEACHING SUGGESTION: Emphasize that the receivers need to run and "fake out" the defenders in order to get themselves in a position for a catch. Likewise, emphasize "man-to-man" defensive coverage for the defenders.

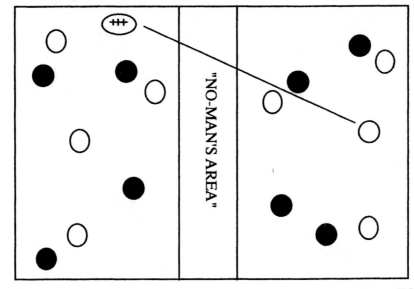

TEAM 1 - ○
TEAM 2 - ●

BOOM IT OVER

SKILL OBJECTIVES: Punting; catching

EQUIPMENT: 2-10 footballs; cone markers

GAME SETUP: With the cones, mark off a playing area with a dividing line down the middle. Students are split into two equal teams with each team assigned to a half of the field. Each player starts with a football.

HOW TO PLAY: The game objective is to punt a football past the other team's goal line for a score. When punting, a player may run up to the center dividing line but cannot cross it. Opposing players can field a ball, either in the air or on the ground, and punt it back. Add more footballs as the game progresses.

   As a variation for the older or more highly skilled student, have the player punt from the spot where he caught or fielded it. There would be no running forward to get closer to the dividing line.

SCORING: One point for each ball that crosses the opponents' goal line on a roll; two points if it crosses in the air. Have a designated player help keep score.

FIELD GOAL CONTEST

SKILLS OBJECTIVES: Kicking; catching

EQUIPMENT: One football and tee for each group of three students

GAME SETUP: This game can be played outside using a goal post, or inside using designated marks on a wall as your "goal posts." Divide the class into groups of three students each.

HOW TO PLAY: Teams are to place their their kicking tees a designated distance from a goal post or wall. One teammate stands by the goal post or wall and awaits the kicked ball. The other two teammates stand in line behind the tee with the football resting on it. On a starting signal, a player from each team runs forward and attempts to kick the ball through the uprights or wall mark. The teammate waiting for the kick retrieves the ball, runs back and puts it on the tee for the next kicker. The player that kicked the ball runs forward and now becomes the catcher. This rotation continues throughout the game with all players having a chance to kick.

SCORING: A player scores 3 points for his team if he kicks a ball through the uprights or hits a designated wall mark.

TEACHING SUGGESTION: Use only foam footballs if playing indoors.

AEROBIC FOOTBALL KICKING

SKILL OBJECTIVES: Kicking; exercise

EQUIPMENT: One football and kicking tee for each pair of students

GAME SETUP: Group the students into pairs. Each pair needs one football and one kicking tee. This game can be played using an outdoor goal post or inside the gym (using marks on the wall for scoring). Have one student place his tee with the football resting on it about 10-20 yards from the goal post or wall (where his partner is standing as well).

HOW TO PLAY: This game is played very much like the Field Goal Contest (see previous game). The main difference being that there are only two players to a team. As a consequence, this activity calls for much more running, as well as more opportunities at kicking.

  On a starting signal, the player standing behind the tee runs forward and attempts to kick the football through the upright or above the wall mark for a score. The partner retrieves the ball, runs back to the kicking spot, places the football on the tee, and now becomes the next kicker. The player that kicked the ball runs forward and now becomes the retriever. This rotation continues throughout the game.

SCORING: A player scores 3 points for each kicked ball that goes through the goal post uprights or, if inside, hits a designated wall spot. Challenge your students to a higher collective point total each time you play. If keeping score, the team with the highest point total wins.

TEACHING SUGGESTION: It would be advisable to use foam footballs for this game, especially if playing inside the gymnasium. This would reduce the possibility of injury.

FOUR DOWNS

SKILL OBJECTIVES : Passing; catching; hiking; dodging; stance position; defensive play

EQUIPMENT : One football for each game; flags for each player; cone markers

GAME SETUP : Two teams with 3-6 players is ideal. Playing multiple games simultaneously for larger classes. Assign one team to start on offense with the ball. Field sizes of 30-50 yards long and 10-30 yards wide would be appropriate for most grade levels.

HOW TO PLAY : The offensive team starts with the ball on their own goal line. They are allowed four downs to move the ball down the field and score. Only pass plays are allowed. The quarterback is not allowed to run down field nor are there any hand-offs. Any member of the offensive team is eligible to receive a pass. A receiver is "tackled" when a defensive player pulls one of his flags. The ball is put at that spot and the next play begins there. An incomplete pass results in the team trying again from the original spot.

On fourth down, the offensive team must pass. No punting is allowed. If fourth down pass is unsuccessful, the opposing team takes possession of the ball at their own goal line and now has four downs to score.

Defensive players guard the offensive players as closely as possible to prevent receptions. The defensive player assigned to the quarterback is the pass rusher. The pass rusher, after counting out loud for five seconds, can chase the quarterback and pull his flag.

SCORING : A touchdown is called each time a team has a receiver cross the opponents' goal line with the ball. Touchdowns count as six points.

ONE CHANCE FOOTBALL

SKILL OBJECTIVES: Passing; catching; running; hiking; defensive coverage

EQUIPMENT: One football for each game; cone markers; flags for each player

GAME SETUP: Set up a field that is 20-50 yards long and 10-30 yards wide. Divide the class into two equal teams. If possible, try to limit team sizes to 4-6 players.

HOW TO PLAY: Since every play is a fourth down, the objective of the game is to score a touchdown on that one play. One team starts with the ball at midfield. Players are to line up in an offensive position with a quarterback, hiker, and receivers. After the ball is hiked to the quarterback, he can either pass it or run. Players receiving a pass have the same privileges and can pass at any time from any spot and in any direction. There can be an unlimited number of passes on any play, either from behind the line of scrimmage or forward. A touchdown is scored if a player crosses the goal line with possession of the ball.

A play is over when the following has occured: an incomplete pass; an interception; a player with the football has his flag pulled; a fumble; or a player with the football runs out-of-bounds with the ball.

After each play, the opposing team receives the football at midfield for their one chance to score. No kicking or punting is allowed.

SCORING: A touchdown is scored when an offensive player with the ball crosses the goal line without having his flag pulled. A touchdown is worth six points.

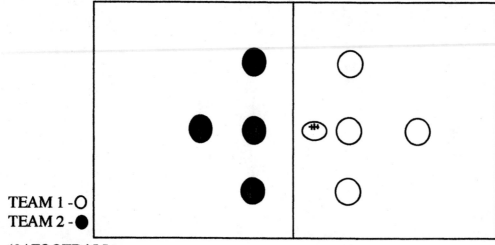

TEAM 1 - ○
TEAM 2 - ●

FLICKER FOOTBALL

SKILL OBJECTIVES: Passing; catching; offensive and defensive play

EQUIPMENT: One football; pinnies for each team; cone markers if playing outside

GAME SETUP: This game can be played either indoors or outside. If outside, mark off a rectangular playing area with the cones. If inside, use the gymnasium floor markings for goal lines. Divide the students into two equal teams with the players scattered throughout the playing area.

HOW TO PLAY: The objective is for a team to have a player catch a pass in the end zone. One team begins with the football on a goal line. Players with the football can't run so the ball can only be advanced down the field by passing and catching. Upon catching a pass, allow a player a couple of steps to stop. He will then have only five seconds to pass it. If not, the ball is awarded to the other team. Opposing players can not get any closer than three yards to either the passer or the receiver. As long as a team successfully catches the football, they have an unlimited number of plays to score. Any ball that touches the ground is awarded to the other team at that spot. A thrown ball can also be intercepted which results in the other team getting the ball at that spot. After a team has scored a touchdown, the other team starts with the ball on their goal line. Remind players to space themselves apart and to play man-to-man defense.

SCORING: A touchdown is scored each time a player has crossed the opponents' goal line with the football. Touchdowns are worth six points.

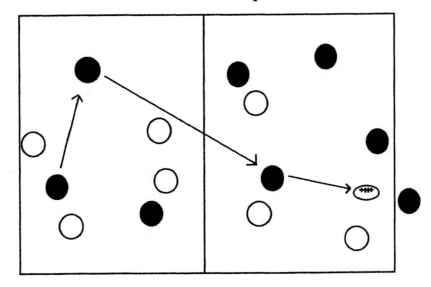

RUN 'N' GUN

SKILL OBJECTIVES: Passing; catching; defensive coverage skills

EQUIPMENT: One football; flags for each player; cone markers

GAME SETUP: Mark off a playing area that's half a normal football field or smaller. Divide class into two equal teams.

HOW TO PLAY: The objective of this game is to pass or run the football across the opponents' goal line for a touchdown. One team starts the game with possession of the ball on its own goal line. The ball can be thrown in any direction. All offensive players can receive a pass and anyone can pass the ball. The ball is advanced toward a goal line by running and passing. If a player with the ball is tagged, he has 5 seconds to pass it to a teammate. If a player with the football runs out-of-bounds, the team in possession throws it in at that spot.

A team is allowed 5 downs to score. An incomplete pass or fumble results in a loss of downs. There is no limit to the number of successful passes a team can make during any given down. An interception results in a turnover, with the other team taking possession at that spot. There is no punting on fifth down, nor are there kick-offs after a touchdown. After a score, the opposite team takes possession of the ball on its goal line.

Encourage the defensive players to play man-to-man coverage, much as in basketball.

SCORING: Each touchdown is worth 6 points.

TEACHING SUGGESTION: Playing multiple games on different fields will result in smaller team sizes and is strongly encouraged.

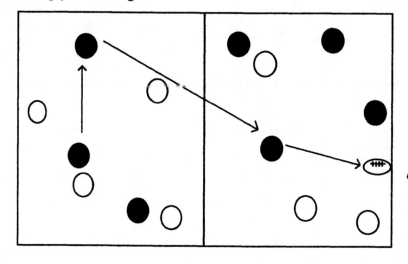

TEAM 1 - ○
TEAM 2 - ●

CHAPTER TWO

SOCCER

SOCCER GAME PROGRESSION GUIDE

GAME	GRADE LEVELS			
	K-2	3-4	5-6	7-8
Mass Soccer	X			
Soccer Red Light - Green Light	X			
Crab Soccer	X	X		
Soccer Maniacs	X	X	X	
Soccer Tunnel Tag	X	X	X	
The Soccer Bull	X	X	X	
Dribble Freeze Tag	X	X	X	
Soccer Pirates	X	X	X	
Pin-Ball Soccer	X	X	X	
Circle Soccer	X	X	X	
Soccer Steel The Bacon	X	X	X	X
3-On-3 Soccer	X	X	X	X
Line Soccer	X	X	X	X
Sideline Soccer	X	X	X	X
Heading Relay Races		X	X	X
Backstop Soccer		X	X	X
Scores Galore		X	X	X
Four Ball Shootout		X	X	X
Soccer Croquet		X	X	X
Rotation Soccer		X	X	X
Four Team Soccer		X	X	X
Modified Soccer		X	X	X

MASS SOCCER

SKILL OBJECTIVES: Most soccer skills

EQUIPMENT: Pinnies and one soccer ball

GAME SETUP: Divide the class into two equal teams with each team lined up on an end line. Place a soccer ball in the middle of the playing area.

This game can be played in the gymnasium or outside on a soccer field.

HOW TO PLAY: Because of its simplicity, this game is great introductory activity for the young and/or less skilled student.

On a starting signal, both teams run forward from their end lines and attempt to gain possession of the soccer ball. The team with possession wants to kick the ball over the opponents' end line, below shoulder level, for a score.

There are no set positions and players are free to roam the playing area. If playing indoors, a no out-of-bounds rule can be implemented by having the ball bounce off the side walls. No one is allowed to use hands. There are no goalies.

SCORING: A team is awarded one point for each ball that crosses the opponents' end line.

END LINE

END LINE

SOCCER RED LIGHT - GREEN LIGHT

SKILL OBJECTIVES: Dribbling, ball control

EQUIPMENT: One soccer ball for each player

GAME SETUP: Divide the class into groups of 4-7 players each; play several games simultaneously if space permits. The caller stands on one line about 15-30 yards from the dribblers who are standing on the starting line.

HOW TO PLAY: This game is played exactly like the popular primary grade level game of Red Light - Green Light with one exception -- players are to dribble a soccer ball instead of running toward the caller.

Select one player to be the caller. He is to stand on one line across from the other players. He can at anytime call out "green light," or "red light." On "green light," the players dribble as quickly as possible toward the caller. On "red light" (and after counting outloud to 5), the caller turns around. Any player not fully stopped with his foot on top of the ball goes back to the starting line. The first player to touch the caller is awarded by becoming the new caller for the next game.

SCORING: There is no scoring. The object of the game is to be the first to touch the caller.

TEACHING SUGGESTION: The ability to control and stop a soccer ball is so important to the success of this game. It is highly recommended that these skills be taught and practiced to a proficient level before the introduction of this game.

CRAB SOCCER

SKILL OBJECTIVES: Kicking; conditioning

EQUIPMENT: Two soccer balls

GAME SETUP: This game is best played in a gymnasium. Divide the class into two equal teams with the players in a crab position. Place two foam soccer balls in the middle of the court.

HOW TO PLAY: On a starting signal, both teams attempt to move one or both of the balls over the opponent's end line while in a crab position. Hands can not be used to hit the soccer ball. After a goal has been scored, the game leader should immediately toss the ball back into the playing area for non-stop action. Since there are no out of bounds in this game, let the balls bounce off the side walls.

SCORING: One point is scored for each ball that crosses the opponents' end line. The team with the highest cumulative score wins.

SOCCER MANIACS

SKILL OBJECTIVES: Dribbling

EQUIPMENT: One soccer ball for each participant

GAME SETUP: This game can be played in the gymnasium or outside with a 50 x 50 feet playing area. With the exception of one player (the "maniac") who is holding the ball in his hands, students are to stand scattered about the playing area with a foot on their soccer ball.

HOW TO PLAY: The objective of the game is to avoid becoming a maniac. On a starting signal, players begin dribbling their soccer ball around the playing area while, at the same time, the player holding the soccer ball (the "maniac") chases after the dribblers attempting to throw and hit their ball.

Players whose soccer balls are hit turn into maniacs themselves. They then try to hit the remaining dribblers' soccer balls. The number of maniacs will grow throughout the game. Stop the game when only one dribbler remains.

SCORING: There is no scoring. Challenge the players to avoid becoming maniacs for as long as possible.

SOCCER TUNNEL TAG

SKILL OBJECTIVES: Kicking, ball control

EQUIPMENT: Enough soccer balls for each player

GAME SETUP: With the exception of the three "Its," all players stand scattered throughout the playing area with their soccer ball on the ground. The three "Its" stand in the center of the playing area, each holding a soccer ball in his hands.

HOW TO PLAY: This fun activity combines dribbling practice with the excitement of a tag game. On a starting signal, the players begin dribbling throughout the playing area. The "Its" chase the dribblers, attempting to throw and hit their soccer balls. If a dribbler has his ball hit by an "It," he retrieves it and stands in a straddle position with the ball held above his head. A tagged player is freed when a dribbler kicks a soccer ball between his legs. Play for 1-3 minutes segments, with new players chosen each time to be the "Its."

SCORING: There is no scoring. Challenge the players to last the entire game without getting tagged.

TEACHING SUGGESTION: When attempting to free a tagged player, encourage the players to dribble in as closely as possible before kicking, and to kick the ball slowly through the player's legs.

THE SOCCER BULL

SKILL OBJECTIVES: Kicking; trapping

EQUIPMENT: One soccer ball for each group

GAME SETUP: Form circles of 8-10 players, with players standing about an arm's length apart. Assign one player to stand in the middle of the circle to be the first "Bull." Before starting, give one of the circle players a ball.

HOW TO PLAY: The objective is to avoid becoming a "Bull." On a starting signal, the circle players try to keep the ball away from the Bull (the player in the middle of the circle) by passing the ball from one player to another. The Bull chases after the ball attempting to intercept or touch the ball with his feet or body. If successful, the Bull switches places with the player who last touched the ball. If the ball goes outside the circle, the player responsible becomes the next Bull.

Emphasize correct kicking and trapping techniques.

SCORING: Challenge the players to avoid becoming a Bull. If keeping score, the player who has been the Bull the fewest times can be declared the winner.

DRIBBLE FREEZE TAG

SKILL OBJECTIVE: Dribbling

EQUIPMENT: Enough soccer balls for all but three players

GAME SETUP: This game can be played in the gym or outside on a playing area that is about 25 x 30 yards in size.

   With the exception of the three "Its" (who do not have a soccer ball), the players are to stand with a foot on their soccer ball.

HOW TO PLAY: On a starting signal, the players begin dribbling randomly within the playing area. At the same time, the "Its" run after and attempt to tag the dribblers. A tagged dribbler is to immediately stop and sit on his soccer ball. He is to stay in that position until touched by a dribbler (thereby freeing him to play again).

SCORING: No scoring. Challenge the players to avoid becoming tagged.

SOCCER PIRATES

SKILL OBJECTIVES: Dribbling; ball stealing

EQUIPMENT: Enough soccer balls for all but 3-4 players

GAME SETUP: Assign 3-4 players to start as pirates (players without soccer balls), with the other players standing throughout the playing area with a foot on top of their ball.

HOW TO PLAY: On a starting signal, the players with a soccer ball start dribbling around the playing area, while at the same time, the Pirates chase after and attempt to steal away a ball. If successful, the Pirate becomes a dribbler and the dribbler (who had his ball stolen) now becomes a Pirate. The objective is to avoid becoming a Pirate.

SCORING: No scoring. Challenge the players to avoid having their ball stolen.

PIN-BALL SOCCER

SKILL OBJECTIVES: Kicking for accuracy; trapping

EQUIPMENT: Six or more bowling pins; six or more soccer balls

GAME SETUP: Form two teams of 5-10 players with teams facing each other on opposite lines that are about 10 yards apart. A row of bowling pins are to be placed in the middle. Each team starts with three soccer balls.

HOW TO PLAY: On a starting signal, the players attempt to kick and knock over as many bowling pins possible (from behind their restraining lines). Players are to trap a ball before kicking. The game leader should retrieve and equally distribute any ball(s) that come to a stop in the middle area. After all the pins have been knocked over, reset and play again.

SCORING: If keeping score, a player that successfully kicks and knocks over a pin is awarded one point.

CIRCLE SOCCER

SKILL OBJECTIVES: Kicking; passing; trapping; blocking

EQUIPMENT: 1-2 soccer balls per game

GAME SETUP: Form two teams of 6-8 players each. Each team stands in a semicircle, with the players a couple of feet apart. One player is assigned to start with the ball.

HOW TO PLAY: On a starting signal, the players attempt to kick the ball below shoulder level past the other team. Opposing players should try to trap the ball before kicking. No hands are to be used during the game.

   If the ball comes to a stop inside the circle, have a player closest to the ball return it back to his spot and kick again. Consider adding a second ball halfway through the game.

SCORING: One point is given to a team that kicks the ball past the other team below shoulder level.

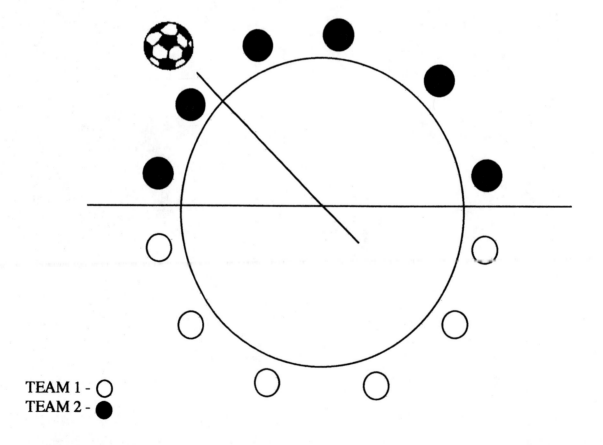

TEAM 1 - ○
TEAM 2 - ●

SOCCER STEAL THE BACON

SKILL OBJECTIVES: Dribbling, ball control

EQUIPMENT: Five hula hoops and four soccer balls for each group of four players

GAME SETUP: Divide the class into groups of four students, with each group given five hula hoops and four soccer balls. Place the four balls into one hula hoop. The other four hula hoops are placed in a square formation around the hula hoop containing the balls. The hula hoops should be spaced 5-10 yards apart. The four players are to start by standing near one of the hula hoops that has designated as their home.

HOW TO PLAY: This game is one that my students have always loved playing. In fact, they would play the entire class period if I let them!

The objective is to have two soccer balls inside your hula hoop. On a starting signal, the four players run to the middle hula hoop (the one containing the soccer balls) and dribble a soccer ball back to their hula hoop. After that, each player attempts to steal a ball from another hula hoop while guarding his own. The game ends once one of the players has two balls inside his hula hoop. Reset the soccer balls and play again.

SCORING: Challenge the players to "steal the bacon" as often as possible. If keeping score, the player that successfully had two soccer balls in his hula hoop the most often after a designated time period could be declared the winner.

TEACHING SUGGESTION: The hula hoops will not slide around as much if you play this game outside on grass. If inside, consider using tape to make circles on the floor as a substitute for hula hoops.

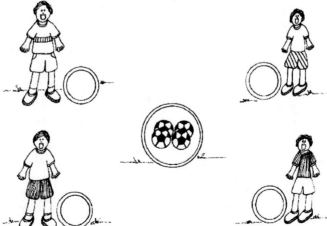

3-ON-3 SOCCER

SKILL OBJECTIVES: All soccer skills

EQUIPMENT: Four cones and one soccer ball for each game

GAME SETUP: Form several small-sized soccer playing areas, with cones used for goals (about six feet apart). Group three players to a team, with two teams assigned to each field. One player from each starts as the goalie with the other two teammates at midfield.

HOW TO PLAY: This game is much like regulation soccer with the exception that only three players are on a team and the field is smaller. Because of the additional ball contact opportunities that this game offers, the players will have plenty of chances to develop the skills of dribbling, kicking, trapping, etc.

The game begins with one team kicking off. Teams try to score a goal by kicking the ball through the opponents' cones. A kick-off follows each score, with players rotating positions. Rotating gives players equal opportunities to play goalie and forward.

Regulation soccer rules apply to hands violations, out-of-bound balls, and rough play.

SCORING: One point for each goal. The team with the highest number of goals wins.

LINE SOCCER

SKILL OBJECTIVES: Dribbling; passing; trapping; kicking; defensive play

EQUIPMENT: One foam soccer ball

GAME SETUP: This game is best played in the gymnasium. Form two teams of equal number. Have the teams each line up on a sideline and number off out loud beginning from either direction. Place a soccer ball in the middle of the court.

HOW TO PLAY: The objective is for the active players (players whose numbers have been called by the game leader) to score by kicking the ball below shoulder level through the other team. The game begins with the game leader calling out two or more numbers. The players on each team with those corresponding numbers run out, try to gain possession of the ball, and attempt to score. The line players act as goalies and are permitted to use hands. If a ball is caught by a linesman, he must pass the ball to one of his active teammates. Linesmen can not punt or score. After each score, call out a new set of numbers.

There are no out-of-bounds. Students play the balls that bounce off the walls and ceiling.

SCORING: One point is scored by a team that has its active players kick the ball past the opponents' linesmen (below shoulder level). Team with the highest score wins.

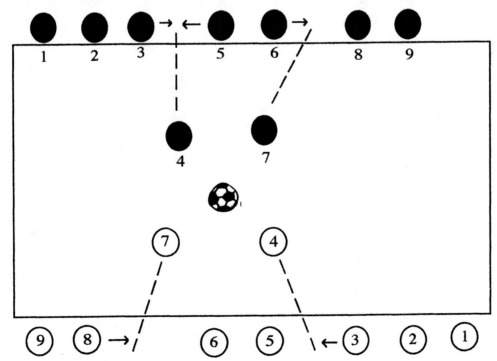

SIDELINE SOCCER

SKILL OBJECTIVES: Dribbling; passing; shooting; defensive play

EQUIPMENT: Four cones; one soccer ball

GAME SETUP: Form two teams of equal number. Half of each team lines up along a sideline and the other half scatters on one side of the playing area. There are no goalie positions in this game.

    Two cones are placed (about 10 feet apart) along each team's end line for goals.

HOW TO PLAY: The game objective is for the active players, aided by their sideline teammates, to score by kicking the ball between their opponents' two cones.

    Play is started by the game leader placing a ball between two opposing players and blowing the whistle. The active players play regular soccer rules with each team attempting to move the ball down the court for a score. Sideline players (who have to stay behind the side line at all times) can pass the ball to their active teammates but are not allowed to score. Following each score the active and sideline players switch places. For a goal to count, the ball must be kicked below shoulder level.

    There are no out-of-bounds in this game, so players should play all balls that bounce off the walls and ceilings. No hands are allowed to be used.

SCORING: One point is awarded to a team that has an active player kick the ball between the opponents' cones. The team with the highest score wins.

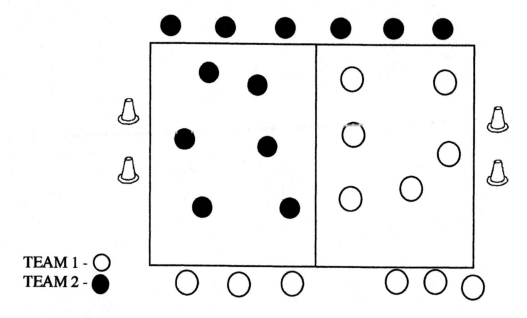

TEAM 1 - ◯
TEAM 2 - ●

HEADING RELAY RACES

SKILL OBJECTIVE: Heading

EQUIPMENT: One soccer ball for each team

GAME SETUP: Set up unlimited teams of 5-8 players each. Have the players stand single file with one player (the server) facing the team and holding a soccer ball.

HOW TO PLAY: On "Go," the server underhand tosses the ball to the first player in line who heads it back to the server and drops to his knees. The server then tosses the ball to the second player who also heads and kneels down. Players continue until the last player has headed and kneeled down. At that point, the server runs to the back of the line and the first player now becomes the server. A team is finished when all players are back into their original positions.

SCORING: The first team to complete the relay wins.

BACKSTOP SOCCER

SKILL OBJECTIVES: Dribbling, passing, defensive play, goalie play, kicking

EQUIPMENT: One soccer ball; pinnies

GAME SETUP: Divide the class into three equal teams. Place one team in front of a baseball backstop to act as goalies. The other two teams start at second base with a kickoff. Designate a line across the backstop as the goal.

HOW TO PLAY: This game is a super choice when you do not have a soccer field available, but you do have baseball backstops. The three team rotation also provides a high level of student participation. Although there are no set positions as in regular soccer, regulation soccer rules still apply to hands and rough play violations.

One team begins with a kickoff from second base. As in regular soccer, the offensive team attempts to score by kicking the ball into the goal (in this case, into the backstop). There are no sset out-of-bound lines, however, a team can only score by kicking the ball into the front of the backstop (the home plate side).

The three teams rotate positions after each score as follows: the backstop goalies move to offense; the team that previously kicked off moves to defense; the team that started on defense moves to the backstop goalie positions. The team with the highest point total wins.

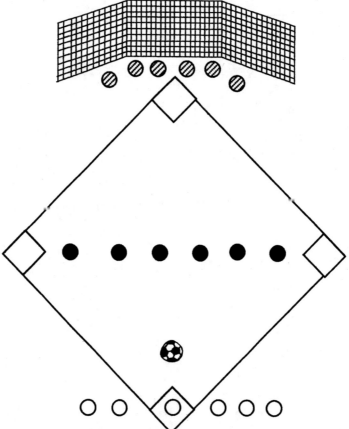

SCORES GALORE

SKILL OBJECTIVES: Dribbling; passing; shooting; defense; goalie play

EQUIPMENT: Eight cones; pinnies; 2-4 soccer balls

GAME SETUP: This game can be played in the gymnasium or outside on a soccer field. Use cones to set up goals on both the end and side lines for each team to attack.

Divide the class into two equal teams, each wearing different colored pinnies. Players can position themselves randomly throughout the playing area. Each team needs two players to play goalie at their designated goals.

HOW TO PLAY: This non-stop action game is great for developing basic soccer skills because of the additional opportunities for players to make contact with the ball.

To start, place two balls in the middle of the playing area. On "Go," players attempt to gain possession of one of the balls and try to score at one of the opponents' two goals. Regulation soccer rules apply to ball handling. There are no out-of-bounds when playing indoors. If outside, use the standard lines as boundaries.

When a goal is scored, the ball is kicked back into action by one of the goalies and play resumes. Each team needs to keep its own score.

SCORING: The team with the highest cumulative score wins.

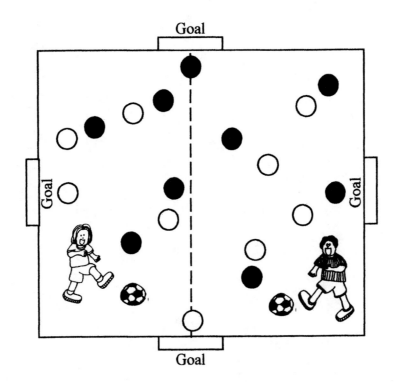

SOCCER / 63

FOUR BALL SHOOTOUT

SKILL OBJECTIVES: All soccer skills

EQUIPMENT: Four soccer balls; pinnies

GAME SETUP: This game can be played inside or outside. Divide the class into two equal teams. Each team should start the game on their own defensive half of the field. Goalies for both teams should be in their goalie boxes. Place four balls on the center line.

HOW TO PLAY: On a starting signal, players attempt to gain possession of the four balls and kick them into the opponents' goal for a score. After the initial start, players are free to roam the playing area (except the goalie box).

When a goal has been scored, the player that made the goal, not the goalie, returns the ball to the center area to kick again. This is a continual action game with all soccer balls played simultaneously.

The goalies are the only players that are allowed to use hands throughout the contest. No players are allowed to enter the goalie boxes except the goalies. Regular soccer rules apply to fouls, hands, etc.

SCORING: Teams score 1 point for each goal. Players keep track of their running score.

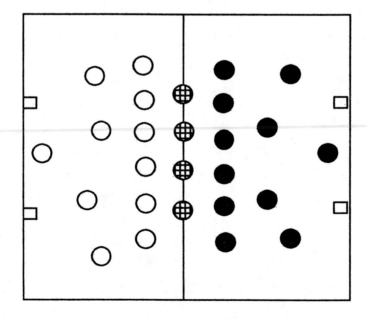

SOCCER CROQUET

SKILL OBJECTIVE: Kicking for accuracy

EQUIPMENT: One soccer ball for each player; 14 cones for each contest

GAME SETUP: Using a soccer field or grassy area, set up the cones as shown below. The course should be laid out as in regular croquet. The size and difficulty of the course can be determined by the age and skill level of the students.

Assign 3-6 players to each contest. Large classes will need several games being played simultaneously.

HOW TO PLAY: This terrific game is played much like regular croquet, except players kick soccer balls between cones (instead of hitting balls with a mallet through wire wickets).

The objective of the game is to be the first player to work his way down to the halfway point, turn around, and return home.

As in regular croquet, the ball needs to be hit (kicked in this case) through the cones going forward before advancing to the next "wicket." Also, everyone has the right to knock someone else's ball with their own.

Players are to stay in the same kicking order throughout the game.

SCORING: If keeping score, the first player to complete the course is the game winner.

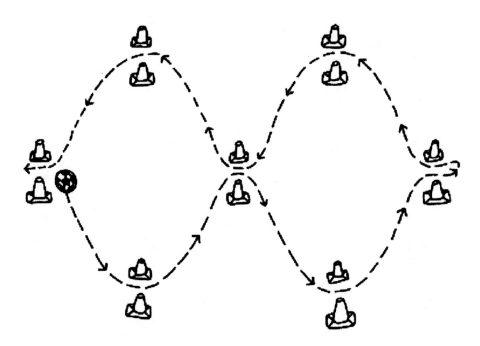

ROTATION SOCCER

SKILL OBJECTIVES: All soccer skills

EQUIPMENT: One soccer ball; pinnies

GAME SETUP: Form two teams of 9 -15 players. Each team is to line up on their half of the playing area in three equal groups of forwards, guards, and goalies (see illustration below). One soccer ball is placed in the center of the playing area prior to the start.

HOW TO PLAY: The objective is for the forwards to kick the ball (below shoulder height) over the opponents' end line. The game starts with a kickoff and all players on their own half of the field. After the kickoff, the forwards are free to play in their opponent's side of the field. The guards are to stay on their half of the field. The goalies are the only ones who are allowed to use hands.

   After each score, players are to rotate positions so all have an equal chance at playing all three positions. The team that was scored against now kicks off.

   Regulation soccer rules apply to hands and rough play violations.

SCORING: One point is scored for each kicked ball that goes past the opponents' end line (below shoulder height).

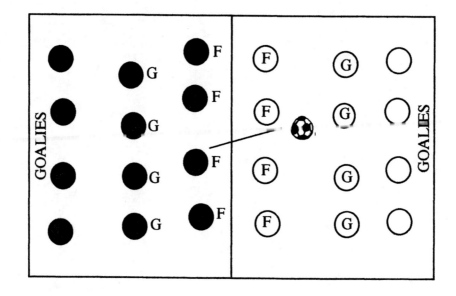

FOUR TEAM SOCCER

SKILL OBJECTIVES: All soccer skills

EQUIPMENT: Two soccer balls; different colored pinnies for all four teams

GAME SETUP: The ideal location for this game is outside on a regulation size soccer field but it can also be played in a large gymnasium. Form four equal numbered teams. Have two teams stand on one side of the field and the other two teams on the opposite side of the center line. Place two soccer balls in the middle of the playing area.

Designate two players whose job it is to stop all shot attempts at the two goals.

HOW TO PLAY: This game pits four teams trying to outscore each other. The game begins with all four teams trying to gain possession of one of the two balls. A team eventually wants to move the ball down the field toward their designated goal and score a goal. Each team scores only at the goal they were facing at the beginning of the game.

After a score has been made, the player making the goal retrieves the ball, brings it back to the center line, and immediately kicks off. At this same time, the other ball continues to be played regardless of what happens.

There are no set positions and players are free to roam the field after the beginning of the game. Player are not to use their hands. Teams are to keep track of the number of goals they have scored.

SCORING: The team with the highest number of goals at the end of a designated time period wins the game.

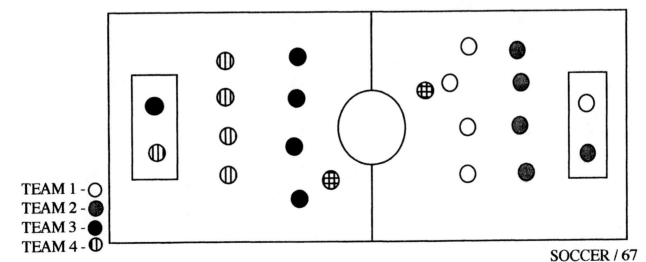

TEAM 1 - ○
TEAM 2 - ◍
TEAM 3 - ●
TEAM 4 - ◫

MODIFIED SOCCER

SKILL OBJECTIVES: All soccer skills

EQUIPMENT: One soccer ball; pinnes

GAME SETUP: Form two teams of 7 players each. Assign players to positions as shown in the illustration below.

HOW TO PLAY: This game is very much like regulation soccer but without the required number of players on the field at one time. Each team has a goalie, three forwards, and three players who play either halfback and fullback. Since the forwards main responsibility is to score points, they should play ahead of the halfbacks/fullback as the ball is moved down the field. After a score, the team scored against kicks off in the center of the field.
  Soccer rules apply for the rest of the game. Penalty and corner kicks should be introduced and implemented for this game. Make sure that players occasionally change positions throughout the game.

SCORING: One point is scored for each goal.

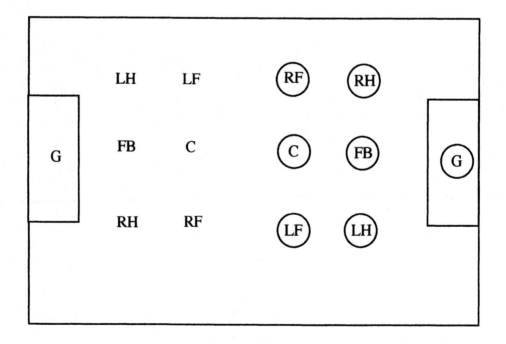

CHAPTER THREE

LACROSSE

LACROSSE GAME PROGRESSION GUIDE

GAME	GRADE LEVELS			
	K-2	3-4	5-6	7-8
Throw & Go		X	X	
Circle Pepper		X	X	
Pass Relay		X	X	
Fly Back		X	X	X
Keep Away		X	X	X
Diamond Run-A-Round		X	X	X
Possession		X	X	X
End Zone Lacrosse	X	X	X	X
Scoop 'Crosse			X	X
Lacrosse Tennis			X	X
Crosse Softball			X	X
Sideline Lacrosse			X	X
Royal Lacrosse			X	X

THROW & GO

SKILL OBJECTIVES: Throwing and catching

EQUIPMENT: Lacrosse sticks; lacrosse ball; two bases

GAME SETUP: The game is best played outside with two bases that are placed 40-60 feet apart. Form two teams of 4 -7 players. Assign a designated catcher for each team. For large classes, play multiple games if space permits.

HOW TO PLAY: The objective is to throw the ball out into the field, run to first base, and return to home base before the opposing team can get the ball to its catcher. Each player on the throwing team gets one chance to throw. A point is scored each time a runner makes it back to home base before the catcher touches home base with the ball in the stick. The number of outs is not counted. Teams are to switch places after all players have had a chance to throw.

SCORING: The team with the highest number of points (after an equal number of innings) wins the game.

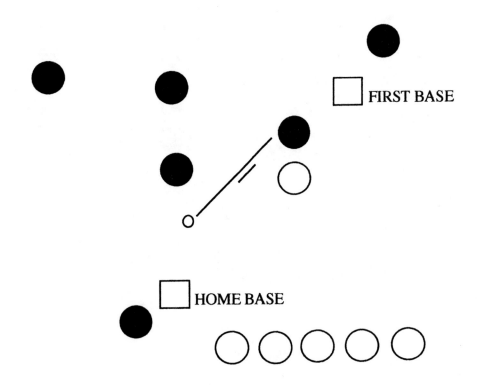

CIRCLE PEPPER

SKILL OBJECTIVES: Throwing; catching

EQUIPMENT: A lacrosse stick for each player, one ball per group

GAME SETUP: Form unlimited teams of 5 -8 players, each standing in a circle formation with one player in the middle. The middle player should start with a ball in his stick.

HOW TO PLAY: The objective is to be the first team to successfully throw and catch the ball around the circle. On a starting signal, the middle player throws the ball to a teammate.

On "Go," the middle player throws the ball to a teammate. That player is to catch the ball either on the fly or by scooping it up, and then passing it back to the middle player. The middle player then throws the ball to the next player in the circle. If a pass is incorrectly handled, play is repeated. This procedure continues on around the circle until everyone has had a chance.

SCORING: If keeping score, the team that successfully finishes first either wins a point or the game.

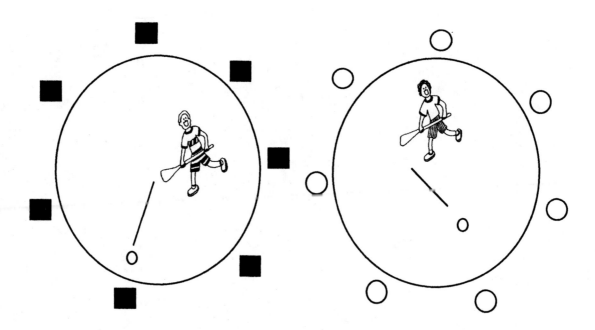

PASS RELAY

SKILL OBJECTIVES: Throwing; catching; running; pivoting

EQUIPMENT: Lacrosse sticks; cone markers; balls

GAME SETUP: Form unlimited teams of 4-6 players. Mark off two lines about 15 -25 yards apart.

HOW TO PLAY: The object of the game is to be the first team back in its original position. The game begins with the first player in each team cradling the ball and running to the designated line. At that time, he is to pivot and throw the ball back to the next player in his line. That player then does the same. Play is finished when the team has returned to its original position.

SCORING: The team that first returns to its original position wins the contest.

TURNAROUND LINE

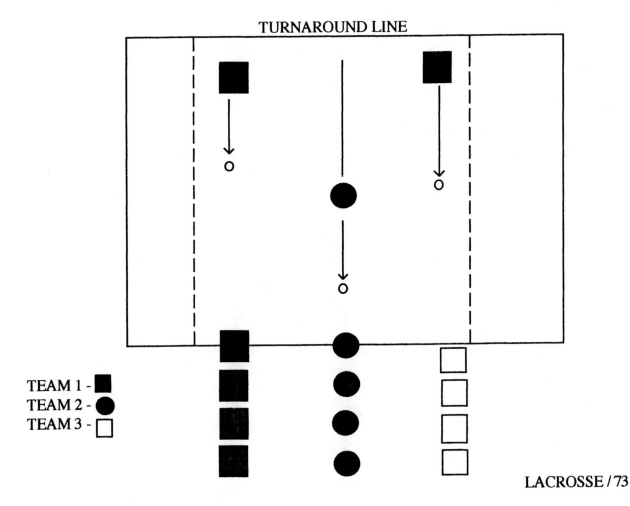

TEAM 1 - ■
TEAM 2 - ●
TEAM 3 - ☐

FLY BACK

SKILL OBJECTIVES: Throwing; catching

EQUIPMENT: Lacrosse sticks; balls

GAME SETUP: Teams of 3-4 players each is ideal. Multiple teams can play at one time.

HOW TO PLAY: The objective is to catch the ball with the stick as many times as possible. The first player in each team stands behind a line which is 10-15 feet away from a wall. This player is to throw the ball against the wall and catch it as many times as possible without letting it hit the floor. His score is the highest number of consecutive catches without a mistake. After the ball hits the floor, the next player takes his place. Play continues for a designated time period.

SCORING: If keeping score, the team that collectively has the highest point total wins the game.

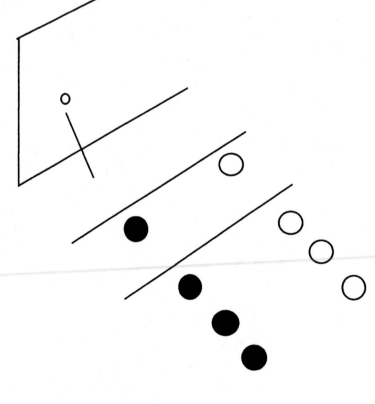

TEAM 1 - ◯
TEAM 2 - ●

KEEP AWAY

SKILL OBJECTIVES: Throwing; catching; guarding

EQUIPMENT: Lacrosse sticks; a ball; pinnies; cone markers

GAME SETUP: Two teams of 5-8 players is ideal. If space permits, try to play multiple games for larger-sized classes. Ask players to guard one player and to stand by that player at the beginning of the game.

HOW TO PLAY: The objective is to keep the ball away from the opposing team and to make successful throws to teammates. The player in control of the ball can not run with it. No defensive player can make contact with a player who has the ball; however, a defensive player can knock a throw down with his stick or intercept it. Defensive players are to guard offensive players, much as in basketball.

SCORING: Score can be determined by one of two ways: the length of time a team has possession of the ball; or the number of completed passes.

TEAM 1 - ○
TEAM 2 - ●

DIAMOND
RUN-A-ROUND

SKILL OBJECTIVES: Throwing; catching; running

EQUIPMENT: Lacrosse sticks; balls; four bases

GAME SETUP: The game is best played on a softball field. Place bases about 30-40 feet apart. Two teams of 6-8 players is ideal. The fielding team starts with a player at each base. The catcher begins with the ball.

HOW TO PLAY: The objective is for the team at home base to have as many players possible run all the bases and return to home base before the fielding team can throw the ball to each base.

To begin, the teacher sets a ball on the ground halfway to first base. On a starting signal the first player on the home team runs and picks up the ball as he heads toward first base. He has to cradle the ball in his stick the entire time as he is running the bases. At this same time the catcher throws his ball to the first baseman. That player throws it to the second baseman, the second baseman throws it to the third baseman, and that player throws it to the catcher. If the fielding team beats the runner home then no point is scored. If the runner beats the throw home, he scores a point for his team. If a baseman fails to catch a throw, another player may field the ball and throw it to the next base. After all the home team players have had a chance to run, the teams are to switch places.

SCORING: One point for each base runner that beats the fielding team's throw to the catcher at home base.

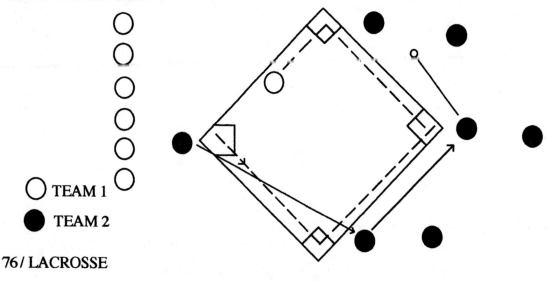

TEAM 1

TEAM 2

POSSESSION

SKILL OBJECTIVES: Throwing, catching, scooping, cradling, and evading an opponent. Stresses the defensive strategy of staying with an opponent.

EQUIPMENT: Lacrosse sticks; a lacrosse ball; pinnies

GAME SETUP: This game can be played either outside or in the gymnasium. A tennis or hand ball can substitute for a lacrosse ball.

    Divide the class into two equal teams. Have the two teams scatter and ready to play man-to-man defense.

HOW TO PLAY: The objective is to pass and catch the ball a higher number of times than the opposing team. Have two opposing players stand in the middle of the playing area. The game leader is to toss the ball in the air between the two players. The player that catches the ball or gains possession will attempt to pass the ball to a teammate without the opponent getting it. A player with possession of the ball has only 10 seconds to run and throw it. If the player takes too much time, the ball is awarded to the opposing team at that spot.

    Defensive players cannot touch the passer or interfere with anyone who is passing the ball. They can, however, intercept the pass. Players going after a ball in the air or on the ground can not push, tackle, or trip another player.

SCORING: Each successful pass and catch counts as 1 point. The team with the highest number of points wins the game. A scoring alternative would be to have 3 consecutive catches count as one point.

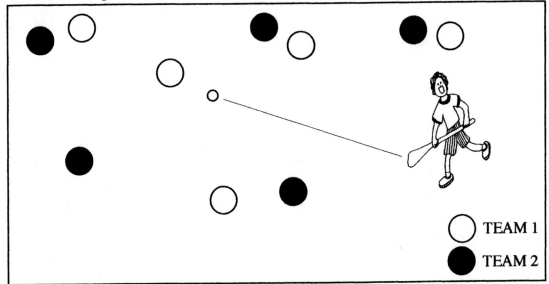

TEAM 1
TEAM 2

END ZONE LACROSSE

SKILL OBJECTIVES: Throwing; catching

EQUIPMENT: Lacrosse sticks; balls; cone markers

GAME SETUP: This game can be played outside or in the gymnasium. Use the cone markers to set up a playing area similar to the illustration below. Divide the class into two equal teams with several players from each team designated as end zone players.

HOW TO PLAY: The objective is for a team to successfully throw a ball to one of its end zone players. The game starts with a fielding player from each team in possession of a ball. This player attempts to throw the ball to one of his end zone players.
End zone players may catch a fly ball or scoop it up successfully for a point. Fielding players can knock down or intercept any throws made by the opposing team. All players must stay in their designated areas until the teacher calls for the players to switch positions. Add more balls as the game continues.

SCORING: One point is scored when a fielder throws a ball into the end zone and it is either caught on the fly or scooped up.

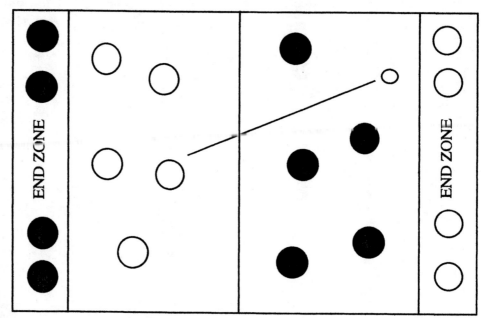

TEAM 1 - ○
TEAM 2 - ●

SCOOP 'CROSSE

SKILL OBJECTIVES: All basic lacrosse skills

EQUIPMENT: Plastic scoops or milk carton boxes (a one gallon plastic milk jug with the bottom half cut off) for each player; one whiffle ball or tennis ball; pinnies

GAME SETUP: Use a regular soccer field if playing outside. For inside, use the basketball court with goal areas.

Form two teams with 6-11 players each. Designate one team to start with the ball first. Each team needs a goalie. The other players are to spread out on their half of the field to start the game.

HOW TO PLAY: This fun game contains many of the elements of regulation lacrosse.

One team starts with possession of the ball at midfield. The player with the ball begins the game by throwing to a teammate. Offensive players attempt to move the ball down the field toward their goal by throwing, catching, and running with the ball. The ball can only be played with the scoop; that is, no hands can be used to scoop a ball up or to catch it. Offensive players are not allowed to throw the ball to themselves.

Defensive players are to guard an offensive player, much as in basketball. Defenders need to be careful not to hit or grab the ball out of an opponent's scoop. This illegal contact would result in a penalty throw (much as a penalty kick in soccer).

Goalies are to stay inside a marked goalie area (the soccer goalie area). No other players are allowed inside this area. The goalie can block a scoring attempt by using their legs or by catching the ball. A ball that is blocked may be picked up by the goalie, put into his scoop, and thrown back into the field of play. If a score is made, the goalie puts the ball back into play again and the game continues.

SCORING: A point is awarded to a team each time the ball is thrown into the goal.

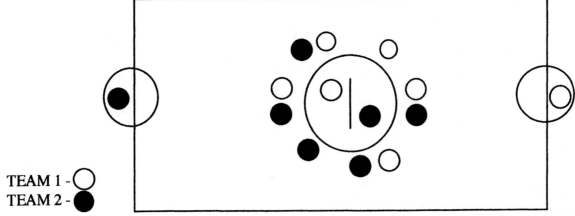

TEAM 1 - ○
TEAM 2 - ●

LACROSSE TENNIS

SKILL OBJECTIVES: Throwing; catching

EQUIPMENT: Lacrosse sticks (or scoops) for each player; one tennis ball

GAME SETUP: Use a regulation tennis court. Form two teams of 3-9 players each. Position the players so that all areas of their half of the court will be covered.

HOW TO PLAY: This game has elements of tennis and volleyball, but lacrosse sticks (or scoops) are used to catch and throw the ball.

The game begins with one team serving. The server stands behind the end line and throws the ball over the net using his stick. The ball is then thrown back and forth until a violation occurs. Both the serve and returns are allowed to bounce once before played by a side. The ball can also be thrown three times among teammates before it has to be returned over the net. No walking with the ball is allowed by the player in possession of the ball.

Violations include: (1) The ball touching the court once it has been played by a side; (2) More than three passes among teammates before the ball is thrown over the net; (3) The ball is thrown out-of-bounds or fails to cross over the net; (4) A player walking while in possession of a ball.

SCORING: Use either regular tennis or volleyball scoring rules.

CROSSE SOFTBALL

SKILL OBJECTIVES: Throwing; catching

EQUIPMENT: Lacrosse sticks; lacrosse ball (or tennis ball); four bases

GAME SETUP: Set up the field as in playing softball. Form two teams of 9-11 players. Designate one team to "bat" first. The fielding team takes softball positions.

HOW TO PLAY: This game is much like softball, with the main exception being that lacrosse sticks are used to throw, catch, and field the ball. Other rule exceptions are: No tagging of baserunners with the sticks; and no stealing of bases.

The pitcher is to pitch the ball underhanded, slow-pitch style. The "batter" catches and then throws the ball anywhere out into the field.

The fielding team can get batting team players out by: striking the batter out; touching the baserunner with the ball (not with the stick); forcing a runner out at a base; catching a fly ball.

Teams are to take turns batting when either three outs have occured or when all members of the batting team have had a chance to catch and run.

SCORING: Same as in softball. One point (a run) is scored when a player successfully circles all four bases.

SIDELINE LACROSSE

SKILL OBJECTIVES: Throwing; catching; goal shooting; offensive and defensive strategy

EQUIPMENT: Lacrosse sticks; goals; one lacrosse ball

GAME SETUP: This game can be played in the gymnasium as well as outside. Divide the class into two equal teams. The teams should line up as shown in the illustration below for the beginning of the game and after each score.

HOW TO PLAY: The objective is to throw the ball into the opponents' goal for a score. To start, the game leader throws a ball between two designated center players who attempt to gain possession by scooping it up with their stick. Players advance the ball toward the goal by running and passing until one player is in position to take a shot at scoring. The scoring attempt must be made beyond the goalkeeper's line. No player can enter this area (except the goalie).

   Sideline players can catch a ball thrown to them but cannot run with it once they have the ball in their stick. They must also remain behind the sideline at all times. After a score and/or a designated time period, the sideline players are to switch places with their teammates.

SCORING: One point for each goal.

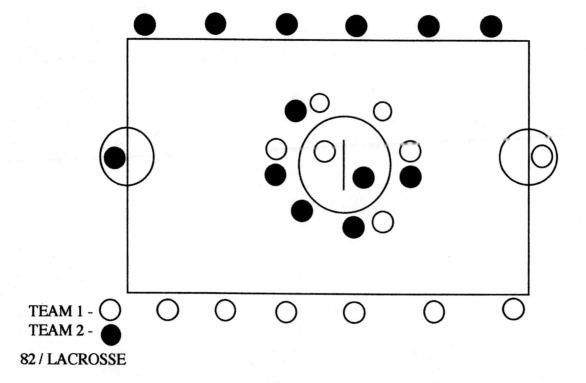

TEAM 1 - ○
TEAM 2 - ●

ROYAL LACROSSE

SKILL OBJECTIVES: Throwing; catching; scooping; defensive guarding

EQUIPMENT: Lacrosse sticks; lacrosse ball; pinnies; cones (if playing outside)

GAME SETUP: Two teams of 5-7 players is ideal. For large classes, play multiple games if space permits. Game can be played either outside or inside. If inside, use basketball floor markings for a playing area.

HOW TO PLAY: The objective is for a team to maintain possession of the ball and have it passed to a teammate in the end zone for a score. A designated team begins with the ball a few yards from a back end zone line. From there, they begin passing and play offense as long as they maintain possession. For the other team to take possession, they must either intercept the ball or scoop up a missed pass.

A goal is scored when the offensive team completes a pass to a player across the end zone line. After a score, the opposing team takes possession of the ball near its goal line and goes the opposite direction.

SCORING: One point for each goal that is made by a player catching a ball in the end zone.

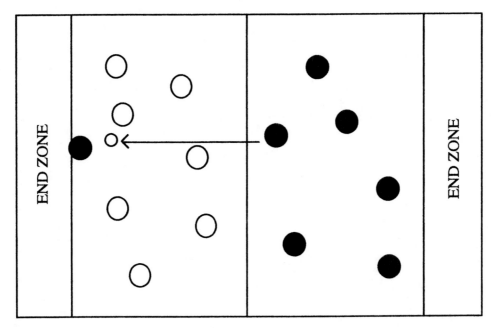

TEAM 1 - ◯
TEAM 2 - ⬤

CHAPTER FOUR

BASKETBALL

BASKETBALL GAME PROGRESSION GUIDE

GAME	GRADE LEVELS			
	K-2	**3-4**	**5-6**	**7-8**
No Rules Basketball	X			
Basketball Pirates	X	X	X	
Gotcha!	X	X	X	
Bull In The Ring	X	X	X	X
King of the Dribblers		X	X	X
H-O-R-S-E		X	X	X
Around The World		X	X	X
Twenty-One		X	X	X
Runners & Gunners		X	X	X
Five Passes		X	X	X
Pass Ball		X	X	X
Basketball Golf		X	X	X
End Zone Basketball		X	X	X
Knock Out		X	X	X
Half-Court Basketball		X	X	X
Three-On-Three		X	X	X
Triple Play		X	X	X
Basket Bordenball		X	X	X
Sideline Basketball		X	X	X

NO RULES BASKETBALL

SKILL OBJECTIVES: Shooting; dribbling; passing; offensive and defensive concepts

EQUIPMENT: One basketball for each game; pinnies

GAME SETUP: Form two teams of 4-6 players. For larger classes, try to play several games simultaneously on different courts.

HOW TO PLAY: This is a fun game for the younger and less skilled student. It's basketball with as few rules possible.

Assign one team to start with the ball from their backcourt area. The players are allowed to dribble, walk, or run with the ball and can take as long as they want to move the ball down the court. No traveling or double dribble violations exist in this game so players have freedom in how they choose to move with the ball.

Players on defense are not allowed to take a ball from an offensive player, nor are they allowed to touch or foul a player. Defensive players can only get the ball off a rebound, a dropped ball by an offensive player, or an interception of a pass.

There are no free throw shots. Violations such as fouls or rough play result in a team throwing the ball in from out-of-bounds. Alternate throw-ins on joint possession calls.

SCORING: A successful shot counts as two points. The team with the highest point total wins.

TEACHING SUGGESTIONS: It's not suggested that this game be played with those grade levels where dribbling is being emphasized.

BASKETBALL PIRATES

SKILL OBJECTIVES: Dribbling ; stealing

EQUIPMENT: Enough basketballs for all but 3-5 players

GAME SETUP: Designate 3-5 players to be "Pirates." These players do not have a basketball. The other players are to stand with a basketball scattered throughout the playing area.

HOW TO PLAY: On a starting signal the players without a basketball (the Pirates) chase the dribblers and attempt to steal their basketballs. Once a dribbler loses his basketball to a Pirate, he becomes a Pirate. A Pirate can not steal a ball from the player who stole it from him. Players with a basketball have to dribble continuously throughout the game using legal dribbling techniques.

SCORING: No scoring. Challenge the players to last as long as possible without losing their basketball to a Pirate.

GOTCHA !

SKILL OBJECTIVES: Dribbling; stealing

EQUIPMENT: One basketball for each player

GAME SETUP: All players start with a basketball and are to stand scattered throughout the playing area.

HOW TO PLAY: On a starting signal, the players are to dribble within the playing area, while at the same time, trying to knock away other player's basketballs with their free hand. Players continuously dribble throughout the playing of the game. Players yell out "Gotcha" when they knock away someone's ball and receive one point for doing so. If a player has his ball knocked away, he is to quickly retrieve it and rejoin the game.

SCORING: One point for each knock away of another player's basketball.

TEACHING SUGGESTIONS: Since this is a very tiring game, it is advisable to play several one minute contests to provide a quick breather in-between.

BULL IN THE RING

SKILL OBJECTIVES: Passing; catching; guarding

EQUIPMENT: One basketball per group

GAME SETUP: Form unlimitied groups of 6-8 players. Have the groups stand in a circle with one player (the "Bull") in the middle of each circle.

HOW TO PLAY: On a starting signal, the players begin passing a basketball back and forth among themselves without the player in the middle (the "Bull") touching or intercepting it. When a ball is touched, the player who last touched it switches places with the "Bull." Players can not throw a pass to the player to the right or left of them, nor can they throw it to the player who threw it to him. Emphasize that chest and bounce passes are to be used.

SCORING: Challenge your students to avoid becoming a Bull.

KING OF THE DRIBBLERS

SKILL OBJECTIVES: Dribbling; stealing

EQUIPMENT: One basketball per group; cones

GAME SETUP: Form unlimited teams of three players each. Have the players on each team begin by lining up behind a cone marker. The cones are placed in a relay type fashion at one end of a basketball court.

HOW TO PLAY: The game starts with the first player in each line dribbling a basketball anywhere around the gym. The second player, on a signal, runs out and attempts to steal away the ball from the first player. When successful, the player who lost the ball goes back to his team's cone while, at the same time, the third player runs out and attempts to steal the ball from the second player. This rotation continues throughout the game.

SCORING: There is no scoring. Challenge the players to last as the dribbler for as long as possible.

H-O-R-S-E

SKILL OBJECTIVE: Shooting

EQUIPMENT: One basketball for each player

GAME SETUP: Assign groups of 2-4 players to play at one basketball goal. Players are to decide a shooting order.

HOW TO PLAY: The objective is to make a shot and hope that the next player in the designated shooting order misses it. When a player makes a shot, the next player has to make the exact same shot. The following players must also make that shot as long as the player ahead of him made it. When a player misses a shot that the previous player had made, he receives the letter "H." The next time he would get an "O" and so on. Once a player misses a shot, the next player in line can shoot from anywhere. A player is out of the game once H-O-R-S-E has been spelled against him. Play continues until one player remains.

SCORING: The last player remaining in the contest (without H-O-R-S-E spelled against him) is the winner.

AROUND THE WORLD

SKILL OBJECTIVE: Shooting

EQUIPMENT: One basketball per game

GAME SETUP: Use one goal with the floor marked as shown in the diagram below. Assign 3-4 players to play against each other. Each group needs one basketball. Players are to decide a shooting order.

HOW TO PLAY: The first player has two attempts to make a shot from spot #1. If successful, he moves to spot #2 and does the same. He keeps advancing as long as he makes a shot with one of his two attempts. When a player misses both shots, the ball goes to the next player in turn. A player can choose not to take the second shot attempt at any time. This results in him being able to start there at that spot when he gets his next chance rather than having to start from spot #1. The objective is to be first player in the group to complete the journey from spot #1 to spot #8, and then back again.

SCORING: The first player to successfully complete the course from spot #1 to spot #8, and back to spot #1, wins the contest.

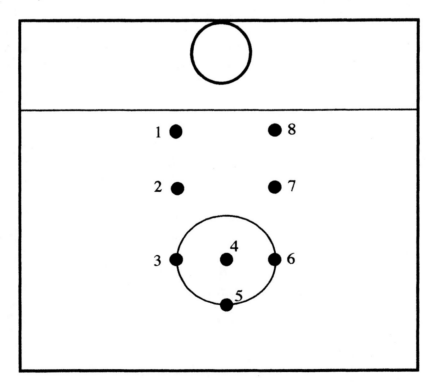

TWENTY-ONE

SKILL OBJECTIVE: Shooting

EQUIPMENT: One basketball for each game

GAME SETUP: The game is played with a group of 3-5 players for each basketball goal available. Each group starts with one basketball. The players are to decide a shooting order.

HOW TO PLAY: The game begins with each player, in turn, taking a long shot and a follow-up shot. The long shot is taken from anywhere behind the free throw line and is worth 2 points if made. The follow-up shot is taken from the spot where the ball is recovered after the long shot and is worth one point if made. If a player makes both shots, he starts with the long shot again and continues to shoot until he misses. A missed shot always results in the next player in line having a chance to shoot.

SCORING: The first player to reach 21 points wins. An alternative scoring method would be to count the number of players within each group that scored 21 points in a designated time period. The group with the highest number would win.

RUNNERS & GUNNERS

SKILL OBJECTIVES: Shooting; dribbling

EQUIPMENT: One basketball per player

GAME SETUP: Divide the class into two equal teams. One team (the dribblers) is to line up on a sideline with each player holding a basketball. The other team (the shooters) is to stand close to the basketball backboards with each player holding a basketball.

HOW TO PLAY: On a starting signal, the shooters try to score as quickly as possible while at the same time, the opposing team runs and dribbles as fast as possible around the outside of the basketball court. Each of the shooters is responsible for keeping track of the number of baskets he has made (one point for each basket). When the last of the dribblers have run 3 laps, stop the contest. Have the shooters now switch places with the dribblers and begin the contest again.

SCORING: The team with the highest number of baskets (after both teams have had the opportunity to shoot) is declared the winner.

FIVE PASSES

SKILL OBJECTIVES: Passing; catching; pivoting; guarding

EQUIPMENT: One basketball per game; pinnies

GAME SETUP: Use half a basketball court for each game. Two teams of five players is ideal. Before starting, players should pick out an opponent to guard during the game.

HOW TO PLAY: Designate one team to throw the ball in first from along a sideline. The objective is to complete 5 consecutive passes, which results in a point. A successful throw-in counts as the first of the 5 passes. The teams are to observe regulation basketball rules in terms of traveling, fouling, and ball handling. A foul results in a free throw attempt, which can score a point. The defensive team can intercept or knock down a pass, but can not touch the offensive player who has the ball.

The offensive team must observe the following rules: A) The ball can't be passed to the player from whom it was received. B) No dribbling is allowed. C) The player with the ball can not hold it for more than 5 seconds. D) A team has only 5 seconds to in-bound a ball from out of bounds. Any of these violations results in the other team taking possession of the ball.

SCORING: One point for each successful execution of 5 consecutive passes and for each successful free throw shot made. The team with the highest point total wins the game.

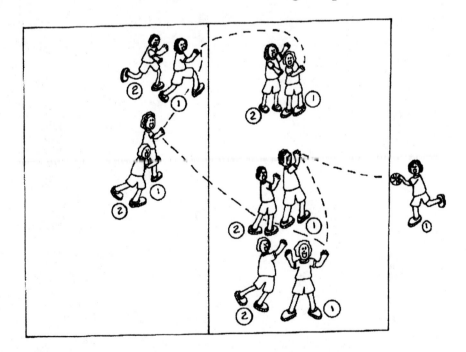

PASS BALL

SKILL OBJECTIVES: Passing; catching; guarding

EQUIPMENT: Several basketballs; cones; pinnies

GAME SETUP: This game is played on a basketball court with a middle neutral zone area marked off with cones. Divide the class into two equal teams. Have half of each team stand on one side or the other. Players should stand by a member of the other team that they will guard throughout the game.

HOW TO PLAY: The objective is to successfully pass the ball to a teammate on the other side of the neutral zone for a point. Dribbling is allowed and players can make multiple passes on one side before passing over the neutral zone. However, only passes that are caught from across the neutral zone count as points. No player can enter the neutral zone.

Defensive players can knock down passes or intercept the ball but are not allowed to touch a player with the ball. Guarding is the same as in basketball. Add more basketballs to the game as time passes.

SCORING: One point is scored for each successful catch made from a pass from across the neutral zone.

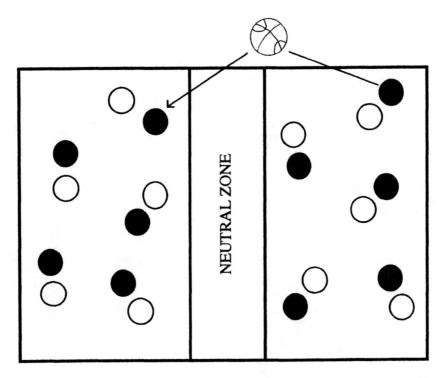

BASKETBALL GOLF

SKILL OBJECTIVE: Shooting

EQUIPMENT: Basketballs; three hula hoops

GAME SETUP: Randomly place three hula hoops on the floor around a basketball goal area with a basketball inside each hoop. Assign three players to a goal. For larger groups, put out more hoops and basketballs to a maximum of six players per goal.

HOW TO PLAY: Players can start at the hula hoop of their choice and all players can begin shooting at the same time. If a player makes his first attempt, his score is one. If he misses, he continues to shoot from that spot, counting 1 point for each attempt. When that player has made a shot, he puts the ball down inside the hula hoop and moves to one of the other hula hoops. When he makes a shot from the new spot, he adds to his previous score. For example, if he had 3 at the first spot and made his first attempt at the second spot, he would now have a score of 4. Play continues until a player has successfully finished all "holes." As in golf, the objective is to have the lowest score possible.

SCORING: Challenge your students to have the lowest score possible. If keeping score, the player with the lowest score wins.

END ZONE BASKETBALL

SKILL OBJECTIVES: All basketball skills

EQUIPMENT: Basketballs; cones or floor tape

GAME SETUP: Set up the playing area with two end zone areas that are marked off with cones or floor tape. Divide the class into two equal teams. Half of each team starts in the end zone and the other half in the court area.

HOW TO PLAY: Begin the game with a jump ball in the middle. The team that gets possession tries to dribble and pass the ball to a teammate in their end zone. The end zone player has one attempt to shoot and make a basket. If he makes it, two points are awarded to his team and the ball is thrown to the court players. The ball is also thrown to the court players if the end zone player misses because only one shot attempt is allowed. End zone players can not leave their end zones. Likewise, court players can not enter the end zones at any time during the game. Basketball rules apply to dribbling and ball handling.

Halfway through the game, the end zone players switch places with their teammates in the court area. Add several additional basketballs throughout the playing of the game.

SCORING: Two points is awarded for each basket made by an end zone player. The team with the highest score at the end wins the game.

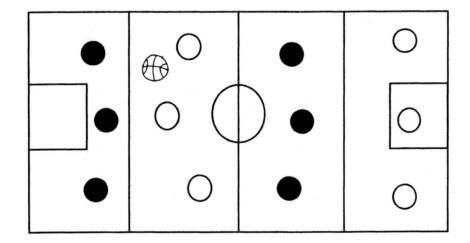

TEAM 1 - ◯
TEAM 2 - ●

KNOCK OUT

SKILL OBJECTIVE: Shooting

EQUIPMENT: One basketball for each player

GAME SETUP: Divide the class into groups (the number dependent on how many baskets are available). An ideal number of players at one goal is 3-5. Have each group stand at their free throw line, with the first two players holding a basketball.

HOW TO PLAY: On a starting signal, the first player shoots from the free throw line. The second player in line does the same immediately after the first player has shot. If the first player makes a shot, the ball is quickly given to the third player in line and the first player goes to the back of the line. The third player now tries to make a basket before the second player does.

   If the first player misses his first shot, he rebounds his shot and continues shooting until either he makes a shot or the second player has made a basket. If the second player makes a basket before the first player, the first player is "knocked out" and must exit the game. The remaining players continue playing with "knock outs" occuring whenever a player makes a basket before the player ahead of him.

SCORING: The winner is the last player remaining that has not been knocked out.

TEACHING SUGGESTIONS: Have an unoccupied goal available for players who have been knocked out to practice shooting. This way, players are kept active.

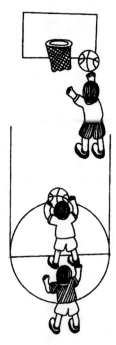

HALF-COURT BASKETBALL

SKILL OBJECTIVES: Shooting; dribbling; passing; defense

EQUIPMENT: One basketball per game

GAME SETUP: As the name implies, the game is played on half a court using one basket. The standard out-of-bound lines on the court apply with the mid-court line being an out-of-bounds line. With floor tape or using the free throw line, designate a neutral zone as illustrated below. Assign two teams to a court with ideal team sizes being 2-4 players each.

HOW TO PLAY: This game is played very much like regulation basketball with the same rules that govern dribbling, fouling, penalties and scoring. The exceptions are:
1) Instead of a jump ball to start the game, designate one team to throw the ball in from the center circle. Alternate throw-ins with each joint possession that occurs during the game.
2) Personal fouls do not result in free throw shooting. The team with the ball throws the ball in from the closest out-of-bounds line.
3) After each score, the alternate team takes possession of the ball at the center circle.
4) After a missed shot and a rebound by the opposite team, no shot can be attempted until that team has had a teammate stand with the ball (with at least one foot) in the neutral zone.

SCORING: A team recieves two points for every basket made. The team with the highest point total at the end of a designated time period wins. Alternatively, the winning team can be the first one to score a designated point total.

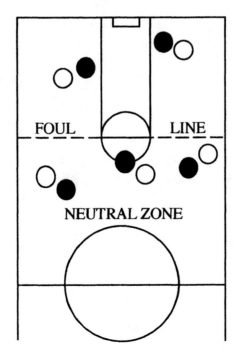

FOUL   LINE

NEUTRAL ZONE

THREE-ON-THREE

SKILL OBJECTIVES: All basketball skills

EQUIPMENT: One basketball

GAME SET: This game is played using a half-court. Divide the class into teams of three players each. Assign three teams to one court. Place two teams on the court ready to play each other, with the third team standing on a sideline.

HOW TO PLAY: This game is played very much like half-court basketball with the exception that a third team rotates into the game after each score. The game begins with one team throwing the ball in-bounds from the top of the court. The objective is to score as in regulation basketball. All rules governing dribbling and ball handling are the same as in regulation basketball. Once a team has been scored against, they are to switch places with the team that has been waiting on the sideline.

There are no free throw shots for fouls that are committed. The other team simply throws the ball in from the nearest out-of-bounds.

SCORING: The team with the highest score at the end of a designated time period wins.

TRIPLE PLAY

SKILL OBJECTIVES: All basketball skills

EQUIPMENT: One basketball per game

GAME SETUP: Divide class into groups of three players each. Assign one group to play at each basket.

HOW TO PLAY: This game is played very much like half-court basketball except three players are playing at the same time with each player being his own team. It's basically one-on-one-on-one. The game begins with one player on offense first with the ball. The other two players are on defense until one of them steals the ball or rebounds a missed shot. This player would then become the new offensive player. If an offensive player makes a shot, he continues being the offensive player. If the defensive players force the offensive player to stop dribbling, then the offensive player is forced to shoot from that spot and must do so within three seconds.

SCORING: A player recieves two points for each shot made. The player with the highest point total at the end of a designated time period wins.

BASKET BORDENBALL

SKILL OBJECTIVES: Passing; catching; shooting; offensive and defensive strategies

EQUIPMENT: One basketball; pinnies

GAME SETUP: Divide the class into teams of 5 players each. Ideal situation is 5 vs. 5, but you can rotate a new set of players after every basket or three minutes. Those players not on the court can be sideline players where they can be involved in passing to teammates.

HOW TO PLAY: A jump ball starts the game with two opposing players in the middle of the court. The objective is to score two points by making a shot, just as in basketball. All the rules of basketball apply with the following exceptions:

1) Players with the basketball can not dribble. Allow 1 step to stop.
2) Players with the basketball have only 5 seconds to pass the ball or shoot.
3) Players on defense can not steal the ball from an offensive player when that player has the ball in his hands. A passed ball, however, can be intercepted or knocked down. Enforce the concept of "shadow" guarding where the defensive players stay 2-3 feet away from the offensive players except in the case of a loose ball or rebound.
4) If a loose ball or rebound results in a joint posession between two opposing players, the ball is always awarded to the offensive team.
5) No free throws are shot. "Fouls" will result in the team throwing the ball in from the closest out-of-bounds.
   Rule violations result in a team losing the ball to the other team, which would then in-bound the ball from the nearest out of bounds spot.

SCORING: Two points are awarded to a team that makes a shot. There are no free throw shots.

TEACHING SUGGESTION: This is a great game for developing beginning basketball skills without the stress of dribbling. The game also can reinforce the necessity of teamwork. If two or three players are only passing to each other then try implementing a 5 pass rule before a score can be attempted. My students consider this game one of their very favorites!

GAME ILLUSTRATION
ON NEXT PAGE -

SIDELINE BASKETBALL

SKILL OBJECTIVES: All basketball skills

EQUIPMENT: One basketball per game; pinnies

GAME SETUP: Form two teams with 8-10 players. Half of each team is to start the game on the court and the other half stands along a sideline.

HOW TO PLAY: The game is played very much like regulation basketball with the exception that each team has sideline teammates to pass to. The game begins with a jump ball in the center of the court with each team attempting to move the ball down the court to shoot for points. No team can try scoring unless they have made at least one pass to a sideline player. Sideline players can not shoot the ball. They can only retrieve balls along the sideline and pass to teammates on the court.

Scoring, fouls and rules are the same as in basketball. After each basket, court players switch with the sideline players.

SCORING: Scoring is the same as in regular basketball.

CHAPTER FIVE

HOCKEY

HOCKEY GAME PROGRESSION GUIDE

GAME	GRADE LEVELS			
	K-2	3-4	5-6	7-8
Hockey Pirates	X	X	X	
Circle Race	X	X	X	
Hockey Steal	X	X	X	X
Pyramid Passing	X	X	X	X
Run 'N' Weave	X	X	X	X
Hockey Keep Away		X	X	X
Line Hockey		X	X	X
Ground Attack		X	X	X
Shooting Goals		X	X	X
Lotsa Pucks		X	X	X
Goalies Galore		X	X	X
3-On-3 Hockey		X	X	X
Sideline Hockey		X	X	X
Position Hockey			X	X
Modified Hockey			X	X

HOCKEY PIRATES

SKILL OBJECTIVES: Stick-handling; stealing

EQUIPMENT: Hockey sticks; goggles; pucks

GAME SETUP: Each player is to start with a hockey stick with about two-thirds of the players also having a puck. The remaining third start the game without a puck and are the "Pirates." Players scatter throughout the playing area.

HOW TO PLAY: The objective is for a free player to avoid having his puck taken by a Pirate. On "Go," the Pirates (players without a puck) chase after and try to steal a puck from a free player. If successful, the pirate now becomes a free player and the player who had his puck stolen now becomes a Pirate. The new Pirate then chases after the free players and tries to steal a puck. The game continues in this fashion.

SCORING: At the conclusion of the game, ask which players had their pucks stolen the least often. Challenge the players to avoid having their puck stolen.

CIRCLE RACE

SKILL OBJECTIVE: Stick-handling skills

EQUIPMENT: Hockey sticks; one puck per team

GAME SETUP: Form teams of 6-8 players each. Players stand in a circle with one player in each circle in possession of a puck.

HOW TO PLAY: The objective is for a team to dribble around the outside of the circle and return back to its original position ahead of the other teams. On a starting signal, the first player on each team is to dribble around the outside of the circle as quickly as possible, return to his original spot, and pass the puck to the player on his right. The rest of the team members do the same. The first team to finish is declared the winner.

SCORING: Have several races. Challenge each team to have the highest number of first place finishes.

TEACHING SUGGESTION: A great variation is to have the players weave between each other instead of dribbling around the outside of the circle.

HOCKEY STEAL

SKILL OBJECTIVES: Stick-handling skills and stealing

EQUIPMENT: Hockey sticks; goggles; pucks for half the players

GAME SETUP: Divide the class into two equal teams. If the teams can't be identified by the the color of sticks, then have one team put pinnies on. Designate one team to start with the pucks. Have players scatter throughout the playing area.

HOW TO PLAY: The objective for the team with the pucks is to avoid losing them to the opposing team. At the same time, the objective of the team without the pucks is to steal as many as possible. On a starting signal, the team without the pucks chases after and attempts to steal as many pucks as they can from the team with the pucks. On a stop signal, the players freeze and the captured pucks are counted. The teams then reverse roles and play continues.

SCORING: The team with the fewest pucks stolen wins the game.

PYRAMID PASSING

SKILL OBJECTIVES: Passing; fielding

EQUIPMENT: Hockey sticks; goggles; one puck per team

GAME SETUP: Form unlimited teams of three players each. Teams are to stand in a triangular position with one player starting with the puck.

HOW TO PLAY: The objective is to pass and field the puck as many times as possible within a designated time period. On a starting signal, the player with the puck in each team passes it clockwise to the next player. Players are to count the number of successful fields and passes. Continue playing for a designated time period. The next contest could have the players passing the puck counterclockwise.

SCORING: The team with the highest number of passes at the end of a designated time period wins. Challenge the teams to achieve a higher score with each game played.

RUN 'N' WEAVE

SKILL OBJECTIVE: Stick-handling skills

EQUIPMENT: Hockey sticks; pucks; cones

GAME SETUP: Unlimited teams of 3-4 players. Players stand in a line behind a cone or floor mark with a hockey stick. The first player in each line starts with a puck. Place 3-6 cones in front of each team, about 3-6 feet apart.

HOW TO PLAY: The objective is to be the first team to complete the relay. On a starting signal the first player in each team drives forward with the puck weaving around each cone and back. The next player then takes off and does the same thing as quickly as possible. When each player has had a chance to go three times, the team members sit down and are finished.

SCORING: The team that sits down first after completing their turns wins the relay.

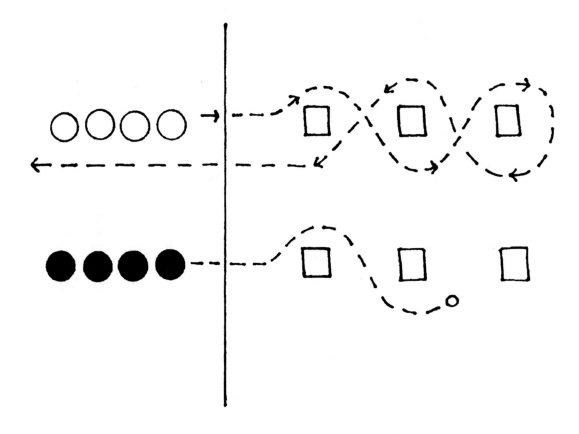

HOCKEY KEEP-AWAY

SKILL OBJECTIVES: Passing; fielding

EQUIPMENT: Hockey sticks and goggles for each player; one puck per circle

GAME SETUP: Divide the class into groups of 7-10 players. Players stand in a circular formation with one player in the middle.

HOW TO PLAY: The objective is to keep the player in the middle of the circle from touching the puck. On "Go," the circle players begin passing and fielding the puck back and forth, while at the same time, the middle player attempts to steal or touch it. If the middle player does touch or steal the puck, the player who last passed or controlled it takes his place in the middle. Play continues in this fashion for a designated time period.

SCORING: At the conclusion of the game, the player within each circle that has been the middle player the least often is declared the winner.

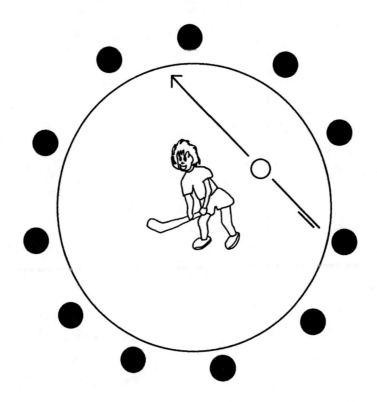

LINE HOCKEY

SKILL OBJECTIVES: Stick-handling; shooting; goalie play

EQUIPMENT: Hockey sticks; goggles; one puck

GAME SETUP: Divide the class into two equal teams with each team standing on a sideline facing each other. Next, have the players number off. One puck is placed in the middle of the playing area.

HOW TO PLAY: The objective is to score more goals than the opposing team. The game begins by the game leader calling out a number. The two players with that number run quickly to the middle, try to gain control of the puck, and attempt to shoot the puck past the opponents' sideline players to score a goal.

The game leader can occasionally call out several numbers. This allows for several players to play at once in the court area.

The sideline players whose number is not called are goalies. They are to stay behind the sideline and defend against shots made by the opponents.

SCORING: One point for a player that successfully shoots the puck past the opponents' sideline players. The team with the highest overall score at the end wins the game.

GROUND ATTACK

SKILL OBJECTIVES: Stick-handling; shooting; passing

EQUIPMENT: Hockey sticks; 10 bowling pins; goggles; 10-20 pucks

GAME SETUP: Set up a rectangular playing area with a center dividing line. Place 5 cones, equally spaced apart, behind each team's end line. Divide the class into two equal teams with each team standing on one side of the center dividing line. Teams are to have an equal number of pucks.

HOW TO PLAY: The objective is for a team to hit their opponents' bowling pins, as well as hit more pucks over the center line. On a starting signal, each team tries to quickly hit as many pucks as possible into the other team's side. They also attempt to shoot and knock over their opponents' pins. At no time can a player cross over the center dividing line. Also, once a pin has been knocked over it can not be set upright again. At the end of a designated time period, stop the game and count the number of points made by each team.

SCORING: Each team receives one point for each puck that is on its side and two points for each pin that was knocked over. The team with the lowest score wins.

TEACHING SUGGESTION: For safety reasons, the game leader should strongly enforce a no high-sticking rule (no blades above the waist). Encourage proper spacing between players as well.

SHOOTING GOALS

SKILL OBJECTIVES: Stick-handling; shooting

EQUIPMENT: Hockey sticks; goggles; marking tape; 2-4 goals

GAME SETUP: Set up two or more goals along a sideline and two or more along the end line. Place a floor marking about 15-20 feet away from each goal. Divide the class into the same number of teams as there are goals available. Each team is assigned to a goal and the players should stand in a line behind the starting spot (which is the marking that is 15-20 feet from the goal). The first player on each team starts with a puck.

HOW TO PLAY: The team objective is to hit more pucks into a goal than the other teams. On a starting signal, the first player from each team shoots from the floor marking for a score. After shooting, he runs forward, retrieves the puck and dribbles it back to the next person in line. Play continues for a designated time. Each team needs to keep track of the number of goals it has made. There are no goalies.

SCORING: Each team recieves one point for each goal that is scored.

LOTSA PUCKS

SKILL OBJECTIVES: Stick-handling; passing; shooting; defense; goalie play

EQUIPMENT: Hockey sticks; goggles; 2-6 pucks; four goals

GAME SETUP: Set up the playing area to include hockey nets at both ends and the middle of both sides. Divide the class into two equal teams. Each team is to have one end goal to defend as well as one side goal. Two pucks are used at the beginning of the game. Goalies stand in front of the goals with the other team members scattered throughout the playing area.

HOW TO PLAY: The team objective is to have the fewest goals scored against it. To begin, have two players from each team (for a total of four) stand in the middle of the playing area. Place two pucks between them. On a starting signal, these players try to gain control of the pucks and pass them to teammates who attempt to score goals at either of the opponents' goals. Add more pucks as the game progresses.

SCORING: The goalies are to keep score of the number of goals that were made against them. After a designated time, stop play and add the points up. The team with the lowest overall score wins.

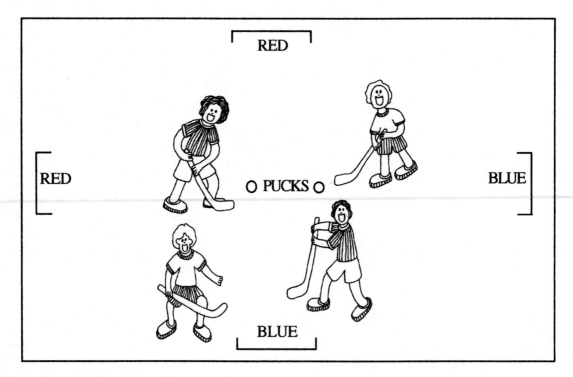

GOALIES GALORE

SKILL OBJECTIVES: Stick-handling; passing; defense; goalie play; shooting

EQUIPMENT: Hockey sticks; marking tape; goggles; one puck

GAME SETUP: Two teams of twelve players each is ideal. Have each team positioned with three forwards, three halfbacks and six goalies. Use a line marking to create an end zone for each team.

HOW TO PLAY: The objective is to hit the puck over the opponents' goal line for a score. The game begins with a face-off between the two center forwards. With their sticks, these two players touch the ground and the opponent's stick three times. Following this, each player tries to get control of the puck or hit it to a teammate. Teams pass and drive the puck back and forth until one team scores a goal by hitting a puck past a goal line. After each goal or a designated time period, players are to rotate (that is, goalies become court players and vice versa).

SCORING: A team is awarded one point each time the puck crosses the goal line. The team with the highest score at the end wins the game.

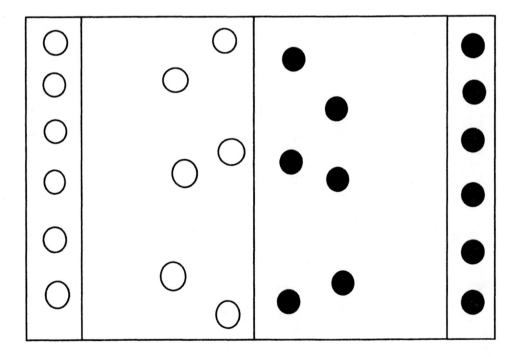

3 ON 3 HOCKEY

SKILL OBJECTIVES: Stick-handling; passing; defense; shooting; goalie play

EQUIPMENT: Hockey sticks; goggles; cones; one puck

GAME SETUP: Using floor tape, mark off several playing areas. Put two cones down at each end of each playing area for goals. Divide the class into teams of three players each. Pair up teams so that you can have several games playing simultaneously.

HOW TO PLAY: The objective is to score more goals than the opposing team. Each team starts with one goalie and two court players. On a signal, each team's court players attempt to get control of the puck and score. Have the puck put back in the middle after each score.

SCORING: One point is scored for each player that hits the puck into the opponents' goal. The team with the highest score at the end of the game wins.

SIDELINE HOCKEY

SKILL OBJECTIVES: Stick-handling; shooting; passing; defense

EQUIPMENT: Hockey sticks; two goals; a puck; goggles

GAME SETUP: Set up goals at the ends of the playing area. Divide the class into two equal teams. Have half of each team stand along a sideline and the other half take positions as shown in the illustration below. Teams have a choice whether to have a goalie or not.

HOW TO PLAY: The objective is to score a goal by hitting the puck into the opponents' goal. The game begins with a face-off in the middle between the two center forwards. They tap the floor and each other's stick three times before trying to gain control of the puck. The teams attempt to pass, drive and score.

Sideline players for each team can help their teams by passing the puck to their court players if the puck goes past the side lines. However, they are to stay behind the side lines and can not run out into the court. They are allowed to score from the sideline.

After each score or a designated time period, the court players are to switch places with their sideline teammates.

SCORING: One point for each puck that a team hits into their opponents' goal. The team with the highest total at the end wins the game.

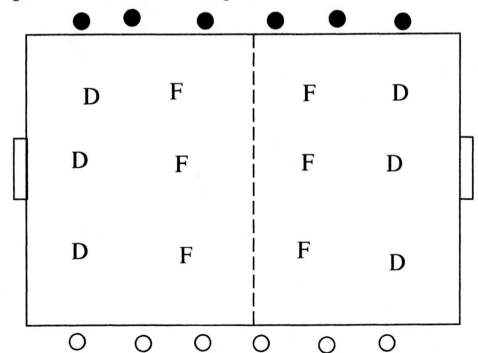

POSITION HOCKEY

SKILL OBJECTIVES: Stick-handling; passing; shooting; defensive and goalie play

EQUIPMENT: Hockey sticks; goggles; two goals; one puck

GAME SETUP: Divide the class into two teams of 6-9 players. For larger classes, play a second game if space permits. Have the players position themselves as shown in the illustration below as either a forward, defensive player, or goalie.

HOW TO PLAY: The game begins with a face-off between two opposing forwards. Players attempt to pass, dribble and score by hitting the puck into the opponents' goal. The forwards and defensive players must stay on their half of the court. That is, the defensive players on team "A" must play on the same half of the court as the forwards on team "B" and vice versa. Players can not cross the center line but can pass the puck back and forth over it.

SCORING: One point for each goal made. The team with the highest score wins.

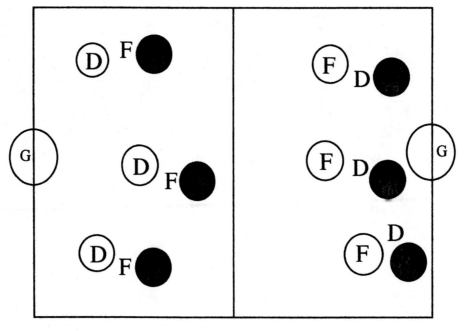

TEAM A- ○
TEAM B- ●

MODIFIED HOCKEY

SKILL OBJECTIVES: All basic hockey skills

EQUIPMENT: Hockey sticks; goggles; cones; one puck for each game

GAME SETUP: Divide the class into two equal teams with 6-10 players each being an ideal number. Assign teams to take positions according to the illustration below. The number of positions can vary depending on the size of the class. For example, two or three goalies are possible if you extend the goal with the cone markers.

HOW TO PLAY: The objective is to score more goals than the opponent. The two center forwards start the game (and after each score) with a face-off. Players pass and dribble until a score is made. There are no out-of-bounds and players can use the entire gym floor.

SCORING: One point for each goal. The team with the highest point total wins.

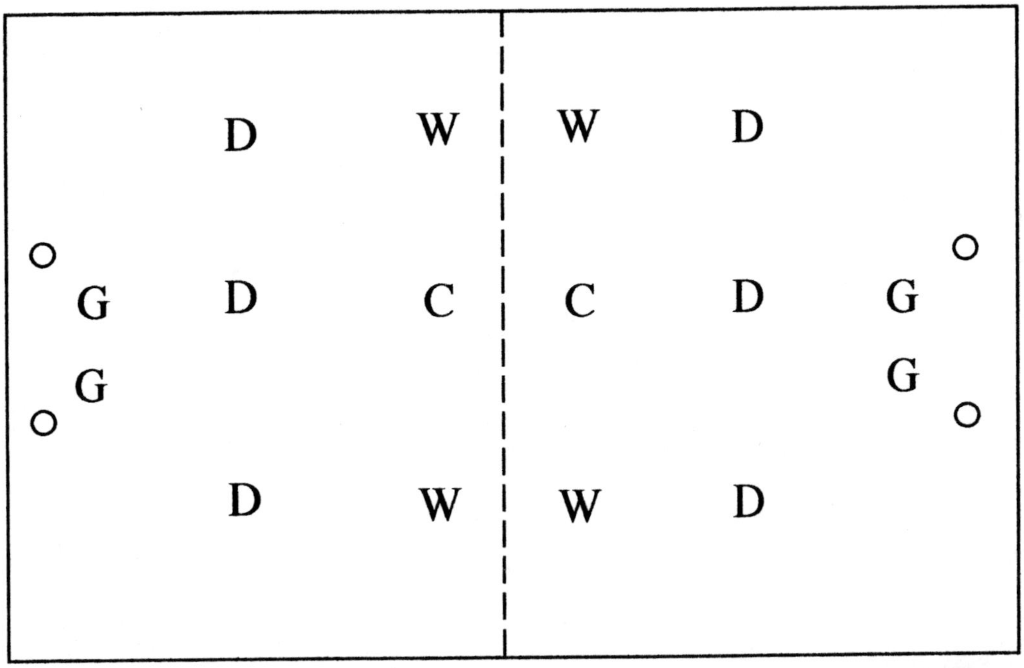

G = GOALIE
D = DEFENSE
W = WING
C = CENTER

CHAPTER SIX

VOLLEYBALL

VOLLEYBALL GAME PROGRESSION GUIDE

GAME	GRADE LEVELS			
	K-2	3-4	5-6	7-8
Catch 22	X	X		
Newcomb	X	X		
Keep It Up	X	X	X	X
No Rules Volleyball		X	X	X
V-O-L-L-E-Y		X	X	X
A-B-C Relay		X	X	X
Air Raid		X	X	X
Serve 'Em Over		X	X	X
Points Galore		X	X	X
Big Ball Volleyball		X	X	X
Hit The Board			X	X
Sideline Volleyball			X	X
Three & Over			X	X
Four-Square Volleyball			X	X

CATCH 22

SKILL OBJECTIVES: Striking; catching; throwing; setting; bumping; serving

EQUIPMENT: One net and 4-6 volleyballs for each game

GAME SETUP: Place two teams, each with 6-9 players, in volleyball court positions as shown below. Each team starts with 2-3 volleyballs.

HOW TO PLAY: This is a wonderful game for the younger and less skilled student. Players are given multiple choices of sending the ball over the net for a possible score. After catching a ball, a player can send it back over the net by serving, throwing, setting or bumping.

   The game begins with each team sending their volleyballs over the net and attempting to make them land on the other team's court. A point is scored each time the ball hits the floor inside the opponents' court area. Players can either catch a ball that comes over the net or volleyball strike it back over. No point is scored for or against a team for sending a ball out-of-bounds. The game is continual with no stopping for points scored and serving.

SCORING: One point is scored each time a team sends a ball over the net and it lands on the other team's court. The first team to catch 22 points wins.

NEWCOMB

SKILL OBJECTIVES: Court positioning; throwing; catching

EQUIPMENT: One net and volleyball for each game

GAME SETUP: Form two teams of 6-9 players. Each team is placed on one side of the net in volleyball positions.

HOW TO PLAY: The game is played very much like regular volleyball except throwing and catching is used instead of volleyball striking. The objective is to throw the ball over the net so that it strikes the floor on the opponents' court, as well as to catch and send back any ball thrown by the opposing team.

  The game begins with a serve (a thrown ball) by one team. Players on the receiving team try to catch it before it hits the floor. After catching a ball, a player is to throw from that spot. No walking with the ball is allowed and a player only has three seconds to throw it. Play continues until one team commits an error by failing to catch a thrown ball or a ball is thrown out-of-bounds. Players are to rotate one court position after every two points.

SCORING: The throwing team recieves one point when an opposing player tries to catch the ball but it drops to the floor. The receiving team recieves one point if a thrower throws the ball out of bounds or into the net. The first team to reach 15 points wins.

KEEP IT UP

SKILL OBJECTIVES: Overhand and underhand volleying

EQUIPMENT: One volleyball for each group

GAME SETUP: Divide the class into groups of 5-8 players each. The players are to stand in a circle formation with one player in each group assigned to start with the ball.

HOW TO PLAY: On a starting signal, the player with the ball tosses it up in the air. The players in the circle attempt to keep it up by striking it with legal volleyball hits. Each contact with the ball counts as a point and the players should keep track of their highest consecutive string of hits. A team has to start back at zero once the ball hits the floor or a player makes illegal contact with the ball.

A player can not hit the ball twice in succession. Emphasize high hits so players can more easily ready themselves to make contact.

SCORING: If keeping score, the team that ends up with the highest consecutive series of hits without an error wins.

NO RULES VOLLEYBALL

SKILL OBJECTIVES: All volleyball skills

EQUIPMENT: One net and volleyball for each game

GAME SETUP: Form two teams of 6-9 players each. Place the teams on each side of the net with one team designated to start with the ball.

HOW TO PLAY: To begin, one team serves. The serve can be done from anywhere on the court. Members of the serving team can help the ball over the net with an unlimited number of assists.

   A team can hit the ball an unlimited number of times before it's returned over the net. A player can also hit the ball to himself an unlimited number of times. Although carries are not called, players are not to catch and throw the ball.

SCORING: A ball must hit on the floor of the opposing team's court to score a point. Both the serving and receiving team can score. The first team to reach 15 points wins.

V-O-L-L-E-Y

SKILL OBJECTIVES: Setting; bumping

EQUIPMENT: One volleyball per group

GAME SETUP: Divide the class into unlimited teams of 3-5 players each. Have each team stand single file about 10 feet from a wall. The first player in each line starts with a ball.

HOW TO PLAY: The game begins with the first player in line set passing the ball against the wall and immediately running to the back of his line. The next player keeps it going using either a bump or set pass. The third player continues to do the same and so on. Whenever a player fails to return the ball up against the wall or fails to make it playable for the next player, he receives the first letter in "volley." When a player has "volley" spelled against him, he is out of the contest.

SCORING: The last player remaining who has not had "volley" spelled against him is declared the winner.

A-B-C RELAY

SKILL OBJECTIVES: Bump and overhand hitting

EQUIPMENT: One volleyball per team

GAME SETUP: Form teams of 5-6 players. Have each team stand single file with one player designated as the leader. The leader starts with the ball and stands about 10 feet away facing the first player in line.

HOW TO PLAY: On "Go," the leader tosses the ball in the air to the first player who immediately strikes it back to the leader. If the first player correctly hits it and the leader catches it before it hits the floor, the team yells out "A." The first player runs to the back of the line and now the leader tosses the ball to the next player in the line. If the second player and leader successfully hit and catch the ball, the team yells out "B." This sequence continues with the leader switching places with a team member after each player in line has been tossed to. The objective is to be the first team to spell out the letters in the alphabet. No letter is awarded for a hit ball that is not legal and/or is not caught by the leader.

SCORING: Each successful hit and catch counts as a letter. Each team attempts to be first to spell out the alphabet.

AIR RAID

SKILL OBJECTIVES: Throwing; catching; volleyball striking skills

EQUIPMENT: Two nets; 12-25 volleyballs

GAME SETUP: Set two nets up to make one long net. Divide the class into two equal teams with each team on a side of the net. Both teams need six volleyballs to start the contest.

HOW TO PLAY: The game leader first designates a particular skill that students must use to get the ball over the net. It can be either throwing, serving, an overhead set, or a bump. Players are to use only that particular skill during the contest.

The objective is to quickly send as many volleyballs as possible over the net by the end of a designated time. The team with the fewest balls on its court is awarded a point.

You can have several "rounds" with a different skill used each time. For example, the first round (lasting 1-2 minutes) can have the skill of serving used to get the ball over the net; the second round can utilize bumping, and so on.

Add more balls during the course of the game.

SCORING: The team with the fewest balls on its side at the end of the time period is given one point. Play several rounds.

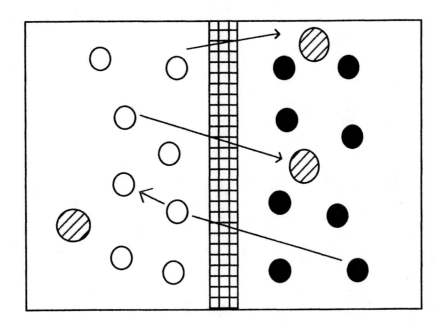

SERVE 'EM OVER

SKILL OBJECTIVE: Serving

EQUIPMENT: One volleyball net and volleyball for each game

GAME SETUP: Have the students stand in volleyball positions, with six players on a team being an ideal number. Designate one team to start with the ball.

HOW TO PLAY: This is a great game for developing serving skills. It's played very much like Newcomb, but rather than throwing the ball over, the players catch and serve the ball over. When a player catches the ball, he is to serve from that spot. No passes are allowed. Players continue serving and catching back and forth until the ball hits the floor inbounds on a court or a served ball goes out of bounds. The team making the error is given one point.

SCORING: The team with the lowest score wins.

POINTS GALORE

SKILL OBJECTIVES: All volleyball skills

EQUIPMENT: One net and volleyball for each game

GAME SETUP: Place two teams of six players on a court in volleyball positions.

HOW TO PLAY: The game is played like volleyball except that a team recieves points for each successful volley, either to a teammate or over the net. Because it's a fast-scoring game, it's best to have a team count out loud their running point total.

The game begins with a serve. If it goes over the net to the other team's side it counts as a point. Successful volleys made after the serve count as points by either team. A point is not gained if the ball hits the floor inside the opponents' court, nor does a hit from a team that goes out of bounds or into the net. A team only receives points for every legal and successful volleyball hit that it makes during the game. The volleyball rule of only two passes being allowed before the ball is to go over the net still applies.

Teams rotate servers and positions after every error by the opposite team.

SCORING: One point for every successful volley, either to a teammate or made across the net. The team with the highest point total after a designated time period wins.

BIG BALL VOLLEYBALL

SKILL OBJECTIVES: All volleyball skills

EQUIPMENT: One volleyball net and one beachball for each game

GAME SETUP: Divide the class into two teams of 6-9 players each. Have the players stand in regular volleyball positions.

HOW TO PLAY: This game is played very much like regular volleyball except that a beachball is used instead of a regular volleyball. Because a beachball is much bigger, a few rules changes are implemented to make the game more successful and enjoyable. They include:
1. Serves can be "helped" over the net by fellow teammates.
2. Players can touch the net during play (but not during a serve).
3. Teams are allowed up to 5 hits to get the ball over the net; individual players are allowed up to 2 hits in a row.
   Other than the above, regular volleyball rules, rotation and scoring are to be followed. This is a super game for the beginning volleyball player. The bigger ball makes it much easier for players to react and make contact.

SCORING: The first team to 15 points wins.

HIT THE BOARD

SKILL OBJECTIVES: Receiving; passing for accuracy

EQUIPMENT: One basketball backboard and volleyball for each group

GAME SET: Divide the class into teams by the number of backboards available. An ideal number is 5-6 on a team. Each team is to stand in a file at the free throw line with one player underneath the goal area facing his team.

HOW TO PLAY: The player underneath the backboard begins the game by tossing the volleyball high up in the air to the first player in line. This player attempts to set or bump the ball up against the backboard. In turn, each player receives a pass from the person doing the tossing and tries to hit the backboard. After all the players have had a chance, the player doing the tossing goes to the back of the line and the first player moves out to become the next tosser. Play continues until the team has returned to its original position.

SCORING: One point for each successful hit made against the backboard. If keeping score, the team with the most points at the end wins.

SIDELINE VOLLEYBALL

SKILL OBJECTIVES: All volleyball skills

EQUIPMENT: One volleyball net and ball for each game

GAME SETUP: Form two teams of 8-10 players each. Have the players stand in positions as shown below, with 4-5 players from each team inside the court and 4-5 players standing along the sidelines and endline.

HOW TO PLAY: This is a great game for large classes or situations where there are too few nets. This game is played very much like regulation volleyball with the exception that extra sideline players are included. The game starts with one team serving and volleyball rules are in effect the entire time. The sideline players can not enter the court area but are allowed to bump or set any ball that comes their way, provided the ball hasn't hit the floor first. A hit made by a sideline player does not count as one of the team's hits. Have the sideline players exchange places with the court players after every 3 points.

SCORING: Volleyball scoring rules are in effect. The team that reaches 15 points first wins.

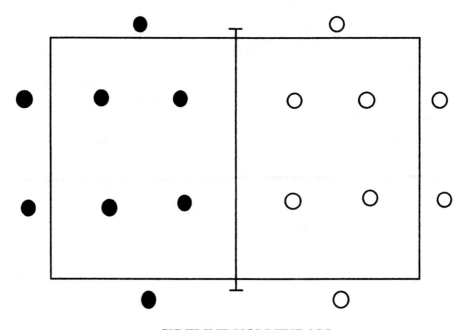

SIDELINE VOLLEYBALL

THREE & OVER

SKILL OBJECTIVES: All volleyball skills

EQUIPMENT: One net and ball for each game

GAME SETUP: Place two teams on a court, one on each side, in volleyball positions. An ideal number is six players on a team.

HOW TO PLAY: Regulation volleyball is played except for the scoring. A point can only be made if a team can volley the ball three times before returning it over the net. Any ball hit over the net before the third hit (even if it hits the opponents' floor) does not count as a point. The scoring is to be ongoing, even during action, every time a team successfully volleys three times.

This is an excellent game for developing setting and passing skills.

SCORING: Score one point for every successful 3 hit volley before the ball is returned over the net. The first team to reach 15 points wins the game.

FOUR-SQUARE VOLLEYBALL

SKILL OBJECTIVES: All volleyball skills

EQUIPMENT: Four volleyball nets; two volleyballs

GAME SETUP: Set up the four nets as shown. Place four equal teams on each of the four courts.

HOW TO PLAY: Designate one team to start by serving into any other court. From then on, the game is played very much like volleyball. Each of the four teams attempts to hit the ball so it lands on the court of another team. One point is given to a team whenever the ball lands on a court or a team commits a volleyball rule violation.

Play continues for an indefinite time period. Consider adding an additional ball halfway through the game so you have two balls being played at the same time.

SCORING: The team that has the lowest score at the end of the designated time wins.

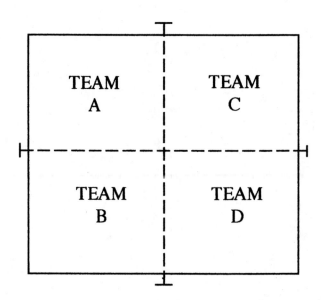

FOUR-SQUARE VOLLEYBALL

CHAPTER SEVEN

BADMINTON

BADMINTON GAME PROGRESSION GUIDE

GAME	GRADE LEVELS			
	K-2	3-4	5-6	7-8
Birdie Relay	X	X	X	
Flying Birdies	X	X	X	
Birdie Keep-It-Up	X	X	X	X
No Net Badminton		X	X	X
Shuttle 'Minton			X	X
Volleyminton			X	X
Mass Badminton			X	X

BIRDIE RELAY

SKILL OBJECTIVE: Striking

EQUIPMENT: Rackets; cones; one birdie per team

GAME SETUP: Form unlimited teams of 3 -4 players each. Set up a playing area which includes a starting line and 3 -6 cones (spaced evenly apart) in front of each team. Teams are to stand single file, with the first player in each team possessing a birdie.

HOW TO PLAY: The objective is to be the first team to finish the relay. On a starting signal, the first player from each team hits the birdie up in the air to himself while running and weaving through the cones. After returning back to the team, he hands the birdie to the next player in line and that player does the same. If the birdie drops to the floor, the player is to pick it up and continue. Action continues until each player has had three turns.

SCORING: The first team to complete the relay wins.

FLYING BIRDIES

SKILL OBJECTIVES: Striking

EQUIPMENT: One badminton racket and birdie for each player

GAME SETUP: A playing area with a net is ideal, but a court with a floor marking down the middle of the playing area will work as well.

   Divide the class into two equal teams. Each team stands on its half of the court.

HOW TO PLAY: The objective is for a team to have fewer birdies on its side than the opposing team (thus, a cleaner court at the conclusion of play).

   On a starting signal, all players begin hitting their birdies over the net (or center line). The more quickly the players are able to retrieve and strike the birdies back over the net, the better chance they'll have of winning. At the end of a designated time period, players are to stop and the number of tennis balls on each side are counted.

   To prevent hitting others with a racket, warn all players to keep enough space between themselves.

SCORING: Challenge the teams to have the fewest birdies on its side. Play several times.

BIRDIE KEEP-IT-UP

SKILL OBJECTIVE: Striking

EQUIPMENT: One racket and birdie for each player

GAME SETUP: Form teams of 4-6 players. Each team stands in a circle with one player in each team assigned to start first with the birdie.

HOW TO PLAY: The objective is to have more consecutive hits in a row without a mistake than the other teams. On "Go," the player with the birdie hits it to the other players in the circle the players are to "keep-it-up" as long as possible. The players are to keep track of their highest number of consecutive hits.

SCORING: The team with the highest number of consecutive hits wins the contest.

NO NET BADMINTON

SKILL OBJECTIVES: All badminton skills except slam shots

EQUIPMENT: One racket and birdie for each player

GAME SETUP: Mark off a court the same size as a regulation badminton court. The game can be played outside or inside. As the name of this game implies, there are no nets. Place 4 players on a court (2 vs. 2).

HOW TO PLAY: Basically, this game is regular badminton with one big exception—there are no nets. This game is particularly helpful when a teacher has enough space but not enough nets to go around.

   Since there is no net, slams are not allowed. The birdie must always be hit with an upward projectory. Otherwise, regular badminton rules apply for doubles play.

SCORING: Regular badminton scoring rules.

SHUTTLE 'MINTON

SKILL OBJECTIVES: Serving; striking

EQUIPMENT: Badminton rackets for each player; one birdie

GAME SETUP: Form two teams of 6-8 players each. Have the players form two lines at each baseline, as shown in the illustration. Groups A and B are one team, while groups C and D make up the other.

HOW TO PLAY: The objective is to hit the birdie back and forth more times in a row than the opponents.
  The game begins with the first player in groups A and C serving a birdie to their teammate (the first player in B and D) and running around the net to the back of that group. After returning the birdie, the players in B and D run around the net to the opposite side. Players try to keep the rally going as long as possible. It helps when the players count out loud the number of hits made.

SCORING: The team with the highest number of consecutive hits wins the contest.

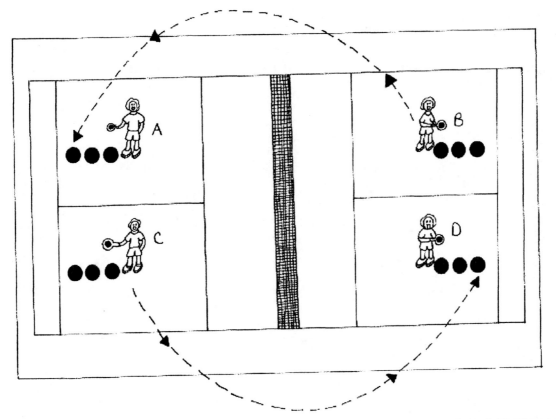

VOLLEYMINTON

SKILL OBJECTIVES: All badminton skills

EQUIPMENT: Rackets; one birdie; one volleyball net

GAME SETUP: Form teams of 6-8 players. Have the players stand in volleyball positions.

HOW TO PLAY: This game is played very much like regular volleyball except badminton striking is used to serve and hit the bird over the net. Play begins with a serve from the player in the right back position. Just as with volleyball, the server keeps serving until a mistake is made by the serving team. When a team loses the serve, the other team then gets a chance at serving and scoring. A team is to rotate clockwise when regaining the chance to serve.

A "side-out" is called and the serving team loses its chance to serve when a violation has occured. If the receiving team commits any of the following, a point is awarded to the serving team:

A) Catching and holding the birdie.
B) A player hitting the bird twice in a row.
C) A team hitting the bird more than three times in a row.
D) Touching the net with the body or racket.
E) Touching the floor on the opponent's side.

SCORING: The first team to 15 points wins the game, provided they have a 2 point advantage.

MASS BADMINTON

SKILL OBJECTIVES: All the skills of badminton

EQUIPMENT: Rackets; one net; one birdie

GAME SETUP: Divide the class up into groups of 3-4 players; this number can vary depending on the number of students and nets. Have one player from each team in a serving position with the remaining team members standing in a file behind the baseline.

HOW TO PLAY: This is an excellent game for those larger sized classes or those situations where not enough nets are available for badminton singles play.

The game begins with a serve from a player in the right service court. Regulation badminton rules are to be followed throughout the game. After the serve, the server quickly leaves the court and runs to the back of his line. The next player in line moves forward onto the court to take his place. After every hit, players are to rotate and this rotation continues until a mistake has been made. Players have only one chance to hit the birdie before they leave the court.

When a player scores a point, the next player in line serves. The receiving player gets to stay on the court to serve when an opposing player has hit the birdie into the net or out-of-bounds.

SCORING: The first team to 11 points, with a 2 point advantage, wins the contest.

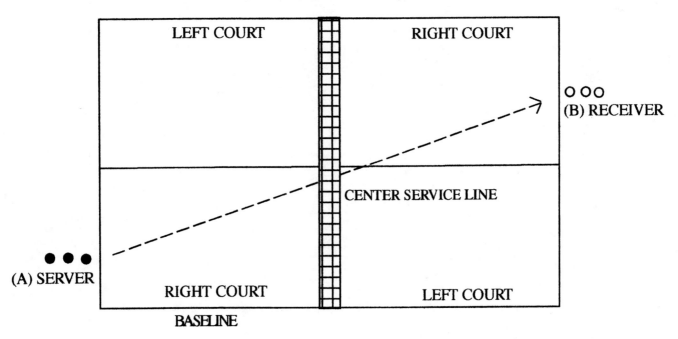

CHAPTER EIGHT

TENNIS

TENNIS GAME PROGRESSION GUIDE

GAME	GRADE LEVELS			
	K-2	3-4	5-6	7-8
Tennis Dribble Relay	X	X	X	
Clean The Court	X	X	X	
Tennis Knock-Out		X	X	X
Floor Ping -Pong		X	X	X
No Racket Tennis		X	X	X
No Rules Tennis		X	X	X
Tennis Keep Away			X	X
Horse Tennis			X	X
Tennis 'Round The World			X	X
Pickleball			X	X

TENNIS DRIBBLE RELAY

SKILL OBJECTIVE: Hand-eye coordination skills with a racket

EQUIPMENT: Rackets for each player; one tennis ball per team

GAME SETUP: Set up relay teams of 3-4 players. The first player in each team starts with a tennis ball. Either use floor markings or cone markers for your starting and turn-around spots.

HOW TO PLAY: The objective is to be the first team to complete the relay. On a starting signal, the first player on each team dribbles a tennis ball (with his racket down) to a designated spot, returns to his team, and gives the ball to the next player in line. A team is finished when each player has dribbled. No player can hold the ball while dribbling. To add to the length of the game, consider having each player go three times before finishing.

SCORING: Challenge each team to finish the relay as quickly as possible.

CLEAN THE COURT

SKILL OBJECTIVE: Striking

EQUIPMENT: One racket and ball for each player

GAME SETUP: Divide the class into two equal teams with each team standing on one half of the court. A playing area with a net is ideal but a floor marking down the middle of the playing area can work as well.

HOW TO PLAY: The objective is to have the fewest number of tennis balls on a court (thus, a "cleaner" court at the conclusion of play).

On a starting signal, all players hit the balls over the net (or center floor line) to the other side. Players are to quickly retrieve and strike the balls back over the net. At the end of a designated time period, players are to stop and the number of tennis balls on each side are counted.

SCORING: At the end of a designated time period, the team with the fewest balls on its side wins. Consider playing several times.

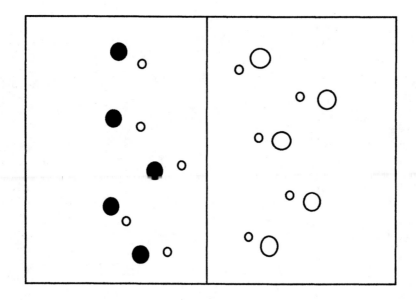

TENNIS KNOCK-OUT

SKILL OBJECTIVES: Striking; serving

EQUIPMENT: Rackets for each player; one ball per group

GAME SETUP: Divide the class into groups of 3-5 players. Each group lines up about 15-25 feet away from a wall. The first player in each line is to start with the ball.

HOW TO PLAY: The objective is to be the last player remaining at the end of the contest. The first player in each line begins by drop serving the ball against the wall and immediately running to the back of the line. The next player in line is to move up and keep the ball in play. The third player, in turn, does the same and so on, until someone misses. A miss counts as one point against a player. A player that is eliminated should have a separate designated area to practice striking rather than be allowed to sit.

SCORING: A player that fails to successfully return a ball gets a point scored against him. After five points, a player is eliminated. The last player remaining is the winner.

NO RULES TENNIS

SKILL OBJECTIVES: Serving; striking

EQUIPMENT: Tennis rackets for each player; one ball per game

GAME SETUP: Form two teams of 2-6 players on a side.

HOW TO PLAY: This is a great introductory game for the younger students and those less skilled.

The game is played like regular tennis with the following exceptions: the serve can be "helped" over the net by teammates any number of times; a player can hit the ball to himself or to a teammate any number of times before hitting it over the net; and a ball may bounce any number of times on a side before it's played.

As long as a ball is bouncing (not rolling), it remains alive and in play. All hits made over the net must land in fair territory.

SCORING: Regular tennis scoring rules apply.

FLOOR PING-PONG

SKILL OBJECTIVE: Striking

EQUIPMENT: Paddles; one tennis ball per game; floor tape

GAME SETUP: Set up courts using floor tape that are 5 x10 feet in size (See the illustration below). Have students pair up and assign two couples to a court.

HOW TO PLAY: The rules are very similar to ping-pong. The game begins with a bounce serve from the right-hand court. The server is to hit the ball with the paddle over the center line and into the opponent's right-hand court. The opponent then returns the ball back anywhere in the opposite court. Players are to continue this, back and forth, until a mistake is made.

Each player serves for five points at a time and then changes to the next player. Teams lose a point if a ball hits on a line or goes out-of-bounds. Failure to return a ball also results in loss of point.

SCORING: First team to 21 points wins.

TEACHING SUGGESTIONS: Remind players that they need to hit the ball upward; no downward hits are to be allowed.

NO RACKET TENNIS

SKILL OBJECTIVES: Scorekeeping; rotation of serving; court positioning

EQUIPMENT: One tennis ball and net per game

GAME SETUP: Have students pair up for teams; assign players to a court with one team (doubles) on each side of the net.

HOW TO PLAY: Basically, this game is tennis without rackets. Players are to catch and throw underhanded throughout the game. However, an overhanded throw can be allowed for the serve. This is an excellent game to teach younger students proper court positioning and how to keep score.

SCORING: Scoring would be the same as in tennis.

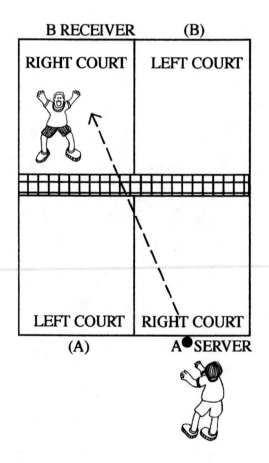

TENNIS KEEP AWAY

SKILL OBJECTIVES: Serving; striking

EQUIPMENT: Rackets and one ball per contest

GAME SETUP: Form two teams with six players each. For larger classes, try to play multiple games if courts are available. Each team is split up with three players on each baseline.

HOW TO PLAY: The objective for the team in the backcourt is to volley a tennis ball back and forth over the net without the opposing team (standing near the net) intercepting or knocking down the ball. The game begins with a player on team "A" serving to his teammates on the other side and attempting to volley as long as possible. Team "B" is to stay in the front court area (near the net and on both sides) and attempt to knock down a pass. After a few minutes, the teams switch places. Each team is to keep track of its highest consecutive number of hits.

SCORING: The team at the end of a designated time period with the highest number of consecutive hits over the net wins the game.

HORSE TENNIS

SKILL OBJECTIVES: Serving; striking

EQUIPMENT: One racket for each player; one tennis ball per game

GAME SETUP: Form groups of 6-8 players. Have each group form two lines at each baseline. Give a tennis ball to the first player in each line (see illustration below).

HOW TO PLAY: The players objective is to have the fewest letters of the word "horse" spelled against him. He does this by making successful serves and returns. The game begins with the first player in line "A" serving to the first player in line "B" and running to the back of his line. The player in line "B" returns the ball over the net and runs to the back of his line. Players are to continue the rally until either a ball is hit out-of-bounds or the returning player fails to hit over the net. The player committing the mistake is given a letter in the word "horse."

SCORING: A player is out when he has received all the letters of the word "horse". Play continues until there is a winner.

TENNIS 'ROUND THE WORLD

SKILL OBJECTIVES: Serving; striking

EQUIPMENT: Rackets for each player; a net; one ball per team

GAME SETUP: Form two teams with eight players each. Have the players from each team form two lines at each baseline. Give a ball to the first player in lines "A" and "C" (see illustration below).

HOW TO PLAY: The objective is to hit the tennis ball back and forth more times than the opponents. The game begins with the player in line "A" drop hitting the ball to the first player in line "B" and running around the court to the end of the opposite line. After returning the ball, the player in line "B" runs around the court to the end of the opposite line. Players are to keep the rally going for as long as possible. It helps when the players count out loud the number of hits made.

The other teams (lines "C" and "D") do the same thing on their side of the court. They should try not to interfere with the opposite team.

SCORING: The team with the highest number of consecutive hits wins the contest.

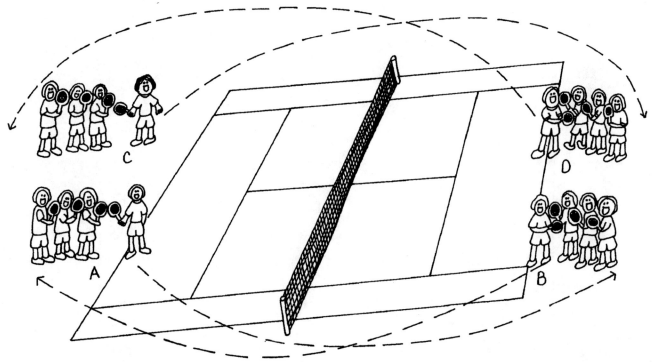

PICKLEBALL

SKILL OBJECTIVES: Serving; striking

EQUIPMENT: Paddles; one net; one pickleball

GAME SETUP: Set up a badminton size court with the top of the net about 3 feet off the floor. Mark off floor lines a few feet from the net on both sides as no-volley zones. Place the students in a "doubles" tennis formation.

HOW TO PLAY: The objective is to score more points against the opponent in the same fashion as badminton, tennis, and other net games. The game begins with a serve below the waist. The ball must land in the diagonal service court. The receiving team lets the serve bounce once before hitting it back. The team that served the ball and receives it again, must also let it bounce once before hitting it. After that exchange, however, both teams can return the ball without letting it bounce.

The "no-volley" zone is the area from the short service line to the net. The ball can bounce in this area, but no player is allowed to return the ball from within that area.

Play continues much as in badminton until an error has occured. Badminton rules and scoring applies.

SCORING: A game is played until one team has 15 points and a 2 point advantage. Only the serving team scores points.

CHAPTER NINE

TRACK & FIELD

TRACK & FIELD GAME PROGRESSION GUIDE

GAME	GRADE LEVELS			
	K-2	3-4	5-6	7-8
Stretch Tag	X	X	X	
Loose 'N' Limber Tag	X	X	X	
Pony Express		X	X	X
Team Cross Country		X	X	X
Hula Hoop Long Jumping		X	X	X
Hula Hoop Discus Throw		X	X	X
Modified Shot Put		X	X	X
Team Olympics		X	X	X

STRETCH TAG

SKILL OBJECTIVES: Jogging; stretching

EQUIPMENT: 3-5 foam balls; cone markers

GAME SETUP: With the cones, set up a corner area big enough for 5-9 students to stretch at one time. Assign 3-5 students to be the first "Its" and to each hold a foam ball. The other students stand scattered throughout the playing area.

HOW TO PLAY: This is a good warm-up game for the sprinting and throwing activities used in track and field. On "Go," the students who have a ball (the "Its") chase the other students and attempt to tag them. An "It" can touch, or throw and hit them with the ball. The student that is tagged goes to the "stretching corner" and performs a series of stretching exercises that have been previously taught. The game leader might want to supervise this area. When finished stretching, the student is allowed to go back into the chasing area.

   Change taggers halfway through the game. The more balls that are used the higher the probability that all the students will be tagged and, thus, spend time stretching.

SCORING: There is no scoring. Students are to try to avoid being tagged.

TEACHING SUGGESTION: Proper stretching techniques need to be introduced prior to playing this game.

LOOSE 'N' LIMBER TAG

SKILL OBJECTIVES: Stretching; jogging

EQUIPMENT: Three foam balls

GAME SETUP: Have the class stand randomly throughout the playing area. Give three students a foam ball and designate them as the "Its."

HOW TO PLAY: This game is played somewhat like *Stretch Tag* with a few differences. The "Its" chase the other students with a foam ball in their hands and attempt to touch the others. "Its" can't throw the ball. They must touch. When a student does get touched, he becomes the new "It." Thus, the "Its" are always changing throughout the game. To avoid getting tagged, students can perform stretching exercises. There are no safe bases for students to escape a tagger. They can only perform the stretching exercises to do that.

It's common for students to get tired when playing tag-type games. Stretching allows them to catch their breath and it has a skill-based twist to it.

SCORING: There is no scoring.

TEACHING SUGGESTION: This game assumes that prior stretching techniques have been introduced to the students. Make sure the stretching exercises you choose for this game are appropriate and safe.

SPRINT TAG

SKILL OBJECTIVE: Sprinting

EQUIPMENT: One cone marker for each pair of students

GAME SETUP: Divide the class into two equal teams. Each player on Team #1 is to stand on a line that is 20-30 yards from Team #2. Each player is to have an opponent directly opposite him. Place a cone marker about 5 yards in front of each player on Team #2.

HOW TO PLAY: On a starting signal, the players on Team #1 jog toward the cone in front of the player opposite him. After touching the cone, the player on Team #1 sprints at full speed back to his starting line. Meanwhile, the player on Team #2 that was directly opposite him attempts to tag the fleeing player before he makes it back to the starting line. Change roles after each race.

SCORING: There are several variations of keeping score. One is to count the number of successful tags after a several races. The team that is tagged least often can be declared the winner.

Players can also compete one-on-one with a partner. Keeping score can be optional.

TEACHING SUGGESTION: Students should be encouraged to use proper sprinting techniques when running to their starting line and when chasing their opponent.

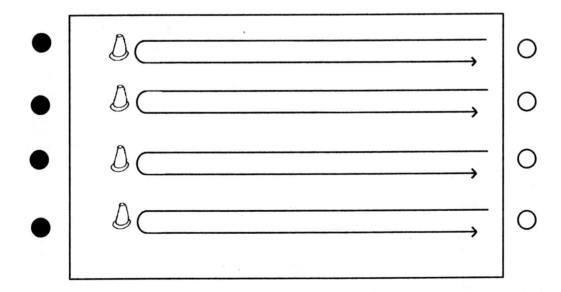

PONY EXPRESS

SKILL OBJECTIVES: Running; baton exchanges

EQUIPMENT: Four batons per team; cone markers

GAME SETUP: Mark off an oval shaped track, much as a real track would look like. Place the cones at four spots along the track, equally spaced apart. Divide the class into teams of 4 players each and assign players from each team to stand at one of these stations. The first runner (at station 1) starts with a baton.

HOW TO PLAY: On "Go," the first runner from each team starts the race by carrying the baton to the teammate at station #2. After handing the baton off, runner #1 stays at station #2. Runner #2 runs to station #3, hands off the baton to the teammate there and stays at station #3. Play continues like this with Runner #4 carrying the baton two spaces to station #2. Every runner at station # 4 will have to do this throughout the playing of the game. The race is finished when all the players are back in their original spots where they began the race. This is an excellent game for practicing correct baton exchanges.

SCORING: The first team back into its originating position is awarded first place.

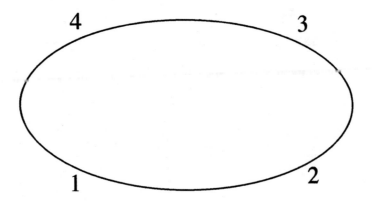

TEAM CROSS COUNTRY

SKILL OBJECTIVE: Running

EQUIPMENT: An outside running area

GAME SETUP: Stake out a 200-400 meter running course or a distance which is appropriate for your age group. Divide the class into teams with 4-5 players each.

HOW TO PLAY & SCORING: On a starting signal, all of the runners begin running. The objective is to run as many laps as possible within a certain time limit. Each runner is responsible for remembering the number of laps completed. After the race, the players are to add up the number of completed laps as a team. The team that has the highest number of completed laps wins the race.

TEACHING SUGGESTION: Try to make sure the teams are fair in terms of running and fitness levels. Have the players come up with a fun team nickname to add to the team "spirit" associated with cross-country running.

HULA HOOP LONG JUMPING

SKILL OBJECTIVE: Standing long jump

EQUIPMENT: Two hula hoops for each pair of students

GAME SETUP: Pair up students with each group receiving two hula hoops. One player stands inside a hula hoop facing a second hula hoop that is 3-5 feet away. The second player awaits his turn to jump by standing beside the jumper.

HOW TO PLAY: This activity will add plenty of student fun and motivation to the practicing of the standing long jump. Start by placing the two hula hoops close together (3-5 feet apart). Using proper jumping techniques which have been previously taught, a player starts by jumping from the first hula hoop to the other. His partner then does the same. With each successful jump have the players move the second hula hoop further and further back (about 6-12 inches each time).

SCORING: Challenge each player to jump further with each attempt. If keeping score, the player that jumps and lands in a hula hoop that is placed furthest away wins. Allow enough time for multiple attempts before stopping the contest.

TEACHING SUGGESTION: To increase their jumping distance, have your students combine their leg thrusts with a strong swing of the arms.

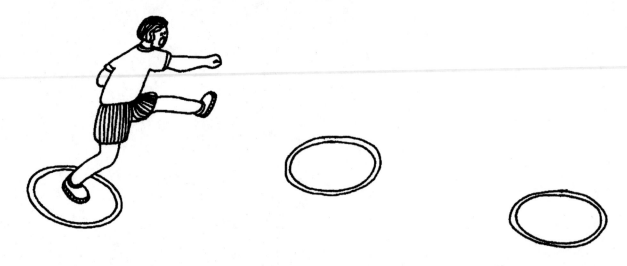

HULA HOOP DISCUS THROW

SKILL OBJECTIVE: Discus rotational throw technique

EQUIPMENT: One smaller-sized hula hoop and cone marker for each pair of students; popsicle sticks

GAME SETUP: Pair up students. Each pair receives one cone marker, two popsicle sticks, and one smaller-sized hula hoop. The cone marker represents a restraining line for the thrower. The popsicle sticks are for measuring the spot where each player lands his hula hoop.

HOW TO PLAY: The hula hoop is a wonderful item to use when introducing the discus throw to your students. In the illustration below, a rotational throw is shown with the player facing the direction of his throw. Following this example, the thrower attempts to throw his "discus" as far as possible. The thrower must stay behind his cone during the throw attempt. The non-throwing partner measures the throw by placing a popsicle stick at the spot where the hula hoop landed. The two players then reverse roles and play continues.

SCORING: Challenge each player to further his throw with each attempt. If keeping score, the player with the longest throw wins. Have the players rotate to new partners after a designated time period or set number of throws.

TEACHING SUGGESTION: Consider using a rubber ring (like the one used in deck tennis) as a discus substitute for those students who have mastered the hula hoop throw.

MODIFIED SHOT PUT

SKILL OBJECTIVE: Glide shot put technique

EQUIPMENT: One ball such as a soccer ball, basketball, playground ball for each pair of students; popsicle sticks for marking spots; cone markers.

GAME SETUP: Pair up students. Each pair receives one cone marker, two popsicle sticks, and one ball. The cone marker represents a restraining line for the thrower. The popsicle sticks are for measuring the spot where each player lands his shot.

HOW TO PLAY: This is great activity for developing the glide technique used in the shot put. Any lightweight ball, such as a basketball, soccer ball, etc., can be used as a substitute for the shot.

  Following the example as shown in the illustration below, the thrower attempts to "put" his ball as far as possible. The thrower must stay behind his cone during the put attempt. The non-throwing partner is to place a popsicle stick at the spot where the thrower's ball landed. The players then reverse roles.

SCORING: Challenge each player to further his put with each attempt. If keeping score, the player with the longest put wins. Have the players rotate to new partners after a designated time period or set number of put attempts.

TEACHING SUGGESTION: You may want to consider using the rotary technique (a full 360 degree turn) with your middle school grade level students. If so, using a softball or similar sized object would be a better choice than the larger ball.

TEAM OLYMPICS

SKILL OBJECTIVES: Track and field skills

EQUIPMENT: Cone markers; stopwatch; medicine ball; beanbags; hula hoops; hurdle equipment; high jump equipment; jump ropes

GAME SETUP & HOW TO PLAY: The following stations require a couple of jumping pits, and a track (or adequate open space) to conduct the events. A teacher can substitute and/or change an event if the equipment or allowable space won't permit it. These listed events assume that the teacher has already previously taught the skills that would be required in order to participate successfully.

Divide the class into the same number of teams as there are event stations. For example, 8 events would mean 8 teams. An ideal number of players on one team would be 3 or 4. Each team needs a designated leader to help keep track of scores.

The game leader is to carefully explain each event to all the participants. Each team will have only 3-5 minutes at a particular event, When the the whistle blows, the teams are to move on to the next event in a clockwise direction.

Station 1, Middle Distance Run: An adequate distance would be one trip around a track or 300-400 meters. All of the runners are to start behind a starting line. On a starting signal, the runners will attempt to complete the route as quickly as possible. As the runners cross the finish line, have a helper read off their times from a stopwatch. Add the individual times together for a team score. The lower the number, the better the team score.

Station 2, Sprint: Players stand in a file behind a starting line. On "Go," the first player runs to a cone about 30-50 yards away, and then back to tag the next player in line. That player does the same and the team continues in this fashion until the whistle has blown. A team scores one point for each round trip.

Station 3, Hurdles: Place hurdles about every 8 -10 yards apart, in a straight line in front of a starting line. On "Go," the players take turns running and jumping over the three hurdles. When a player has jumped the third and last hurdle, he quickly runs back to tag the next runner. It's important that players don't begin until tagged. Teams get one point for each hurdle jumped. A hurdle that is knocked over does not count as a point.

Station 4, Long Jump: The game leader is to place three jump ropes across the pit area for scoring reasons. Players stand in a line about 10-15 yards from the pit. Taking turns, each player runs forward and jumps as far as possible. A player recieves one point for jumping past the first rope; two points for jumping past the second rope; and three points for jumping past the third rope. The leader adds up the points for a team score.

Station 5, Triple Jump: This event is set up exactly like the long jump event. Ropes are placed across the pit. The jumpers take turns and play continues until the whistle has blown. The scoring is the same as in the long jump event.

Station 6, High Jump: Players choose one of three heights when jumping. The lowest height counts as one point; two points for the middle height; and three points for the highest option. Players jump until the whistle has blown. The team leader is to tally the points for each jumper.

Station 7, Medicine Ball Throw: Place three long ropes across a throwing area. The ropes should be placed about three yards apart in front of a throwing line. The players take turns throwing the ball as far as possible. The scoring is similar to the long jump and triple jump events. A player recieves one point for throwing it past the first rope; two points for the second rope; and three points for throwing it past the last rope. When finished throwing, a player retrieves his ball and gives to the next person in line. Play continues until the whistle has blown.

Station 8, Beanbag Relay: An empty box is set in front of the starting line, with four hula hoops spaced every five yards in a row straight out from the box. Each of the hoops contains a beanbag. On the starting signal, the first player in line runs forward, picks up the beanbag in the first hoop, runs and places it in the empty box, and does the same for the remaining beanbags. After bringing the last beanbag back the player tags the next runner in line and goes to the back of the line. The next player is to place the beanbags in the hoops one at a time. Play continues in this way until the whistle has blown. Players recieve one point for each completed round trip. Add up the points for a team total.

Alternative Event Suggestions:

A) *Baton Relay:* Space each team member about 50 yards apart in a circular pattern. On "Go," the first runner runs toward the second runner with a baton. The second runner takes the baton and runs to the third runner, hands off the baton and so on. After handing off the baton, the runner stays in the spot where he handed it off at. The relay is continual so each runner moves up a spot after handing the baton off. Score one point for each successful exchange of the baton.

B) *Softball Throw:* This event is organized much as in the medicine ball throw. However, the ball will be thrown much further so the ropes (or cone markers) need to be placed further out into the field. A total of five ropes or cone markers would be more appropriate for this event. A ball that is thrown and lands past the first rope would count as one point; two points for landing past the second rope, and so on for the remaining ropes. Add the individual points up for a team total at the end of the event.

C) *5 Minute Run:* (or any time limit you would like to use and is appropriate for the age of the students). The players are to run at the same time and try to complete as many laps as possible within the five minutes. A runner recieves one point for each completed lap. Add the individual points together for a team total.

CHAPTER TEN

SOFTBALL

SOFTBALL GAME PROGRESSION GUIDE

GAME	GRADE LEVELS			
	K-2	3-4	5-6	7-8
Baserunning Relay	X	X	X	
Around The Horn	X	X	X	
Hot Taters	X	X	X	
Grounder Ball	X	X	X	X
In A Pickle	X	X	X	X
Kickball		X	X	
Throw & Go	X	X	X	
Tee-Ball	X	X		
No-Outs Kickball		X	X	
Slugger Ball		X	X	
Throw & Run Softball		X	X	X
One Chance Softball		X	X	X
Add 'Em Up		X	X	X
Long Base		X	X	X
No-Team Softball		X	X	X
Home Run		X	X	X
No-Outs Softball		X	X	X
Three-Team Softball		X	X	X
Modified Slo-Pitch		X	X	X
Mat Kickball		X	X	X

BASERUNNING RELAY

SKILL OBJECTIVE: Running around the bases

EQUIPMENT: Four bases; cones

GAME SETUP: Set up the four bases about 35-50 feet apart. Place a cone on the inside of each base. Divide the class into four equal teams and assign each team to a cone.

HOW TO PLAY: This is a fun activity for developing baserunning techniques and speed. Before starting the game, stress the importance of angling out when approaching a base.
    On a starting signal, the first runner in each team runs counter clockwise around the four bases (touching each one) and returning back to his team to tag the next player in line. The objective is to be the first team to complete the relay.

SCORING: Challenge the teams to be the first at completing the relay.

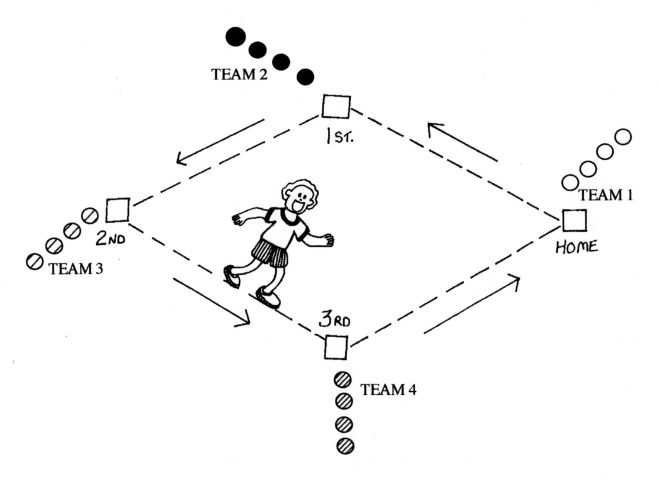

AROUND THE HORN

SKILL OBJECTIVES: Throwing; catching; baserunning

EQUIPMENT: Bases; one softball

GAME SETUP: Set the bases in a diamond-shaped formation. Form two teams of eight players each. The fielding team has two players at each base. The baserunning team starts behind home base.

HOW TO PLAY: The game starts with a runner standing on home base and the catcher holding the ball. On "Go," the catcher throws the ball to first base and on around the other bases while, at the same time, the runner attempts to run around and touch each base. The fielding team has to throw the ball "around the horn" twice while the runner has to only circle the bases once. If the baserunner beats the ball home he has scored one point for his team.

When the ball is being thrown around the horn, one fielder takes the first throw and the second fielder takes the second throw. Fielders can not interfere with the baserunner and must touch each base before throwing to the next base.

Switch sides when each member of the running team has had a turn.

SCORING: One point for each runner that beats the ball being thrown around the bases twice. The team with the highest number of points wins.

HOT TATERS

SKILL OBJECTIVES: Throwing; catching

EQUIPMENT: Gloves; one softball per group

GAME SETUP: Form unlimited circles of 6-8 players each. Circles should be large enough so that players can safely react to overhand throws. Assign one player in each circle to start with the ball.

HOW TO PLAY: On "Go," the players begin throwing the ball to different teammates within the circle; with the goal of being the first team to throw and catch the ball 25 times. The player with the ball can not throw to the player who threw it to him, nor may he throw it to a player on his sides. With each successful catch, the players should count out loud their team score. A dropped ball does not count toward the required 25 catches.

SCORING: Challenge the teams to be the first at successfully making 25 catches.

TEACHING SUGGESTION: Consider doing this same relay by having the students throw underhanded, or by throwing and catching grounders.

GROUNDER BALL

SKILL OBJECTIVES: Batting ; fielding ground balls

EQUIPMENT: Cones; gloves; two bats; one softball

GAME SETUP: Form two teams with 4-6 players each. Place a line with two cones at the end of each line about 30-40 feet apart. Players are to stand on the lines facing each other. Assign one player to bat first.

HOW TO PLAY: This game allows your students to practice catching ground balls. For safety purposes, be sure to have previously taught the correct technique of fielding a ground ball before introducing this game.

The objective is for the batter (who tosses the ball to himself) to drive a ground ball through the opposing team. The ball must hit the ground before crossing the other team's line and it must be directed between the two cones on that line. If the ball crosses the line without being fielded it counts as a point for the batting team.

After a team has had each player bat, the other team then has a team member of its own attempt to hit it across the line the other way. Each player is to take turns at batting.

SCORING: One point for each batted ball that crosses the opponent's line. The team with the highest point total wins.

IN A PICKLE

SKILL OBJECTIVES: Base running; throwing; catching

EQUIPMENT: Two bases; gloves; one ball

GAME SETUP: Divide the class into groups of three players each. Each group needs one ball and two bases that are set about 30 feet apart. Have two players occupy the bases and a third player standing halfway between the two bases.

HOW TO PLAY: A baserunner is in a "pickle" when he is caught between two bases with the possibility of getting run down and tagged. This is a contest to practice the skills of both baserunning and fielding.

The contest begins with the player in the middle trying to reach one of the two bases safely without getting tagged with the ball by one of the fielders. The fielders try to tag the runner by throwing the ball back and forth, running toward him so he can be touched. If the baserunner reaches one of the two bases without getting tagged, he trades places with one of the two fielders. In turn, the players rotate and continue to play in this fashion.

SCORING: Players get one point for each successful attempt to reach a base without getting tagged.

KICKBALL

SKILL OBJECTIVES: Throwing; catching; kicking; baserunning

EQUIPMENT: Bases; a foam soccer ball (or soft playground ball)

GAME SETUP: Divide the class into two equal teams. One team bats first and the other team assumes fielding positions.

HOW TO PLAY: The game is played according to softball rules with the following exceptions:
1) Instead of batting, a soft playground or foam ball is rolled by the pitcher to the batter who kicks it. After the kick, the kicker runs the bases as in softball.
2) The fielding team can put the kicker out by catching a fly ball, tagging the runner in-between bases, throwing and hitting the runner (below the shoulders) with the ball, or forcing the runner out by getting the ball to a base before the runner gets there.
3) No leading-off or base stealing is allowed by the baserunners.
4) There are unlimited outs. Teams switch places after everyone on the kicking team has kicked.

SCORING: One point is scored each time the kicker has safely returned home.

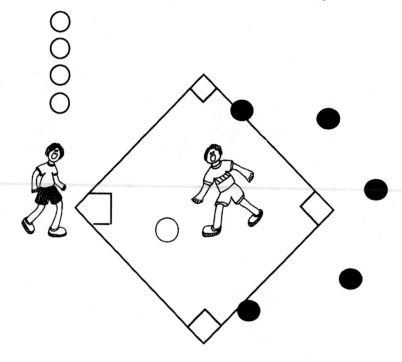

THROW & GO

SKILL OBJECTIVES: Throwing; catching

EQUIPMENT: Lacrosse sticks; lacrosse ball; two bases

GAME SETUP: Two teams of 4-7 players would be ideal. Assign a designated catcher for each team. The game can be played outside or in the gymnasium. Place bases about 40-60 feet apart.

HOW TO PLAY: The objective is to throw the ball out into the field, run to first base, and return to home base before the opposing team can get the ball to its catcher. Each player on the throwing team gets one chance to throw. A point is scored when a runner makes it back to home base before the catcher touches home base with the ball in the stick. The number of outs is not counted. The teams switch places after all the players have thrown the ball.

SCORING: The team with the highest number of points (after an equal number of innings) wins the game.

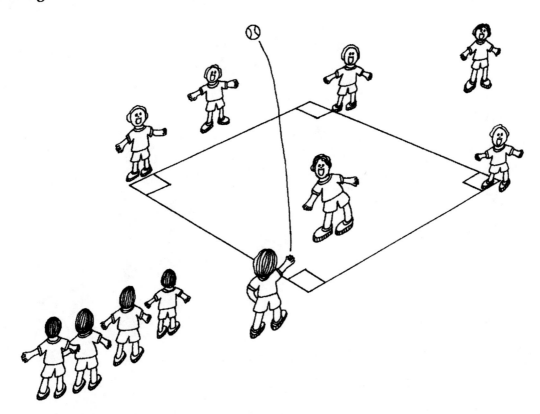

TEE-BALL

SKILL OBJECTIVES: All softball skills except pitching and base stealing

EQUIPMENT: Bases; one bat; one softball; gloves; one batting tee

GAME SETUP: Divide the class into two teams. One team bats first with the other team in fielding positions. Place extra fielders in "rover" positions.

HOW TO PLAY: This is an excellent game for developing batting skills with your younger students. The game is played very much like regular softball with the following exceptions:
1) There is no pitching. Instead, batters are to hit the ball off a batting tee. The tee needs to be adjustable so that it can be raised or lowered for the batter. The catcher places the ball on the tee each time. After the ball is hit, play is the same as in regular softball.
2) There are no strike-outs.
3) No bunting is allowed.
4) No base stealing is allowed since there is no pitching.
5) After 3 outs are committed by the batting team, any baserunners are called out and must go back to their backstop. Teams do not switch places until all batters have had a chance to hit.

SCORING: A team scores one run if a batter runs the bases and safely touches home base. The team with the highest number of runs wins the game

NO-OUTS KICKBALL

SKILL OBJECTIVES: Throwing; catching; kicking; baserunning

EQUIPMENT: Bases; one soccer ball or playground ball

GAME SETUP: This game is played on a regular softball field. Form two teams of 6-10 players each. One team lines up to kick first with the other team in fielding positions.

HOW TO PLAY: This game is played exactly like *No-Outs Softball* except the pitcher rolls a soccer or playground ball to the batter to be kicked.

The object of the game is to kick the ball out into fair territory and run the bases without stopping before the catcher gains possession of the ball and yells out "freeze." This is the signal for the baserunner to stop running and to stay in that position, even if he is not on a base. When the next kicker kicks the ball, the baserunner(s) start running again around the bases until the next "freeze" signal. Each time a baserunner touches home base it counts as a point. The baserunners do not stop after circling the bases once but, instead continue to run and score until everyone on their team has kicked. There are no outs.

Teams switch places after each kicker has had a chance to kick the ball.

SCORING: One point each time a baserunner touches home base. The team with the highest point total wins.

SLUGGER BALL

SKILL OBJECTIVES: Batting; catching

EQUIPMENT: Bases; gloves; one bat; one softball

GAME SETUP: Form two teams of 6-9 players. One team bats first with the other team in fielding positions.

The game is played on a regular softball field with the exception that a restraining line is drawn from third base to first base.

HOW TO PLAY: This is strictly a batting game with no baserunning . The objective is to hit the ball past the restraining line. It's a good substitute for batting practice.

Each batter is given up to three pitches to hit the ball into fair territory past the restraining line. If the ball is fielded without error, the batter is called out. If the ball is not fielded, or fielded incorrectly, then it counts as a successful hit. It's best if the pitcher is a member of the batting team.

The teams switch places when all members of the batting team have had a chance to hit.

SCORING: If the batter hits the ball so it can not be fielded, or fielded properly, and it passes the restraining line, it is considered a hit. He is awarded 1 point if the ball lands in the infield and 2 points if it goes into the outfield.

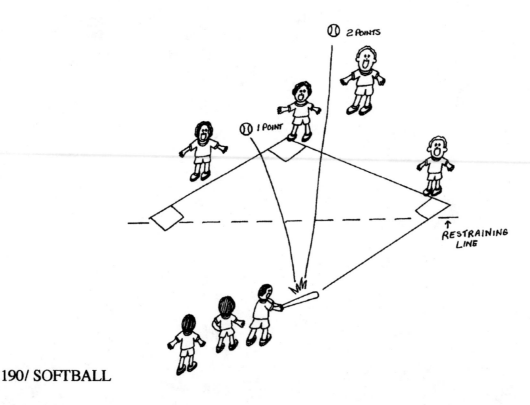

THROW & RUN SOFTBALL

SKILL OBJECTIVES: All softball skills except batting

EQUIPMENT: Bases; one softball

GAME SETUP: Form two teams of 6-10 players each. Assign one team to take fielding positions and the other team to line up in a throwing order.

HOW TO PLAY: This game is played very much like regulation softball except that the batter, instead of batting the ball, catches the pitcher's pitch and immediately throws it anywhere in the field. The ball is played by the fielders as it would be in regular softball.

Specific rules for this game also include:
1) The batter is called out if he drops a pitched ball that is in the strike zone.
2) A ball thrown by the batter into foul territory is considered an out.
3) There is no stealing by baserunners.

SCORING: A team receives one point (a run) each time a team member safely circles the bases.

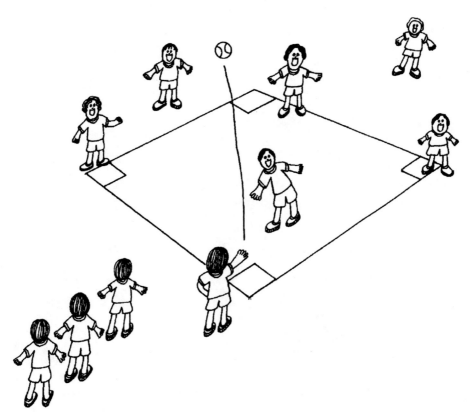

ONE CHANCE SOFTBALL

SKILL OBJECTIVES: All softball skills

EQUIPMENT: Bases; bat; gloves; one softball

GAME SETUP: Form two teams with 6-10 players each. One team lines up in a batting order while the other team takes fielding positions.

HOW TO PLAY: This game is like regular softball except the batter gets only one chance to hit the pitched ball. Because of this, it works best if the pitcher is a member of the batting team.

A batter is out (in addition to regular softball-rule outs) when he swings and misses the pitch or hits a foul ball. There are also no bunts. If a batter does try bunting, he is called out. Baserunners are not allowed to steal bases.

Teams are to switch places when each batter has had a chance to bat.

SCORING: A team scores a run for every baserunner that makes it safely to home base. The team with the highest number of runs wins the game.

ADD 'EM UP

SKILL OBJECTIVES: All softball skills

EQUIPMENT: One bat; one softball; four bases

GAME SETUP: Form two equal teams of 8-10 players with one team batting and the other in fielding positions.

HOW TO PLAY: This game is played very much like regulation softball except for the scoring—which can add up to a lot! Players who hit the ball get 1 point for reaching first base safely; 2 points for getting to second base; 3 points for third base; and 4 points for a home run. The batting team should count out loud their team score when a teammate is running the bases and scoring points. Everyone bats before switching.

    The fielding team can put out a batter if they either catch a fly ball or touch the runner with the ball when he's not on a base. Each batter is allowed three pitches. It works best to have the pitcher be a member of the batting team.

SCORING : A baserunner scores 1 point for reaching first base safely; 2 points for getting to second base; 3 points for reaching third base; and 4 points for home base. The team with the highest score wins.

LONG BASE

SKILL OBJECTIVES: All softball skills

EQUIPMENT: Two bases; one bat; one ball; one batting tee; gloves

GAME SETUP: Place two bases about 30-50 feet away. Form two equal teams with one team batting first and the other team in the field. The fielding team has a catcher and a pitcher, with the other players scattered throughout the playing area.

HOW TO PLAY: The game begins with the pitcher throwing underhanded to the batter. The batter's goal is to hit the ball and make it to the long base or to the long base and back without getting tagged. The batter is out if tagged while running. The batter can choose to stay at the long base if he doesn't think he can safely make it back to home base. In fact, the batter can stay at the long base until there are three baserunners there; then everyone must run on the next hit regardless of how hard the ball is hit.

   Batters can be put out if the fielding team catches a fly ball or if the fielding team tags the runner with the ball.

   There is no stealing or strike outs. A batter has the option of using a batting tee after two strikes.

SCORING: One point is awarded a team that has a runner make it safely to the long base and back home.

NO-TEAM SOFTBALL

SKILL OBJECTIVES: All softball skills

EQUIPMENT: Bases; gloves; bat; one softball

GAME SETUP: Place 7-10 players in softball positions with one player at bat.

HOW TO PLAY: This game is played with regulation softball rules. However, there are no teams. It's every player against everyone else, with each person trying to outscore all the others.

When a batter is out, he rotates to the right field position. The other players rotate one spot as well with the catcher becoming the next batter. (See the illustration below for the player rotation).

A batter continues to bat and run the bases as long as he is successful. A fielder can bypass the normal rotation if he catches a fly ball that a batter hits. In this case, the fielder and the batter would switch positions with each other.

SCORING: Players are to keep their own individual score. Each player should attempt to have the greatest number of runs at the end of the game.

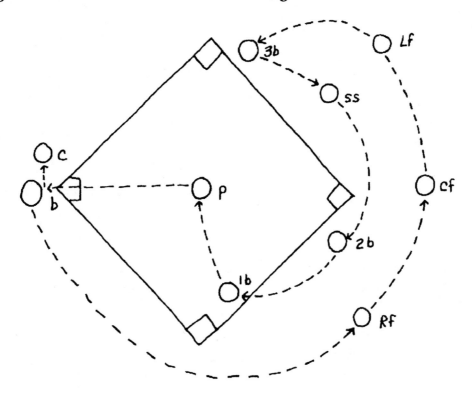

HOME RUN

SKILL OBJECTIVES: All softball skills

EQUIPMENT: Bases; gloves; bat; one softball

GAME SETUP: Form two teams with 5-10 players each. One team bats first with the other team in fielding positions.

HOW TO PLAY: Batters can either be pitched to or they can use a batting tee. After hitting a ball into fair territory, the batter must run and touch each base including home base before the ball gets to the catcher. The fielders attempt to get the batter out by retrieving the ball and throwing it to first, second, third and home base. An out is produced if the ball gets to the catcher, who touches home base before the runner makes it there. Baserunners can not stop at a base or else they are called out. Fly balls, even if caught by the fielding team, must still be played and the ball thrown around the bases. Teams are to rotate after the batting team has had each player bat.

SCORING: A batter scores one point if he hits a home run.

NO-OUTS SOFTBALL

SKILL OBJECTIVES: All softball skills

EQUIPMENT: Bases; gloves; one bat; one softball

GAME SETUP: The game is played on a regular softball field. Form two teams of 6 -10 players each. One team bats first and the other takes fielding positions. It works best to have the pitcher be a member of the batting team.

HOW TO PLAY: The objective for the batter to hit the pitched ball out into fair territory and run the bases without stopping before the catcher gains possession of the ball and yells out "freeze." This is the signal for the baserunner to stop running and to stay in that position, even if he is not on a base. When the next batter hits the ball, the runner(s) start running again around the bases until the next freeze signal. Every time a baserunner touches home base it counts as 1 point. The baserunners do not stop after circling the bases once but, rather, continue to run and score until everyone on their team has batted. There are no outs.

Teams switch places after each batter has had a chance to hit and run.

SCORING: Baserunners receive one point for touching home base.

THREE-TEAM SOFTBALL

SKILL OBJECTIVES: All softball skills

EQUIPMENT: Bases; bat; ball; gloves; one mask

GAME SETUP: Set up a softball diamond with the bases. Form three teams with 4-5 players each.

HOW TO PLAY: This is a great game for a large sized class and for eliminating player waiting time when batting.

The rules of softball apply, with the exception that three teams are competing against each other at the same time. Team #1 begins at bat; Team #2 includes the infield positions of pitcher, catcher, 1st, 2nd, and 3rd base; Team #3 includes the outfield positions of left, center, right fields, and shortstop (and rover if playing with 15 players).

When Team #1 has committed 3 outs, all the teams rotate. Team #1 moves to the outfield positions; Team #2 becomes the next batters; Team #3 moves up into the infield positions.

An inning includes all three teams having a chance to bat.

SCORING: One run for each baserunner that touches home base. The team winning is the one with the highest number of runs after a designated number of innings.

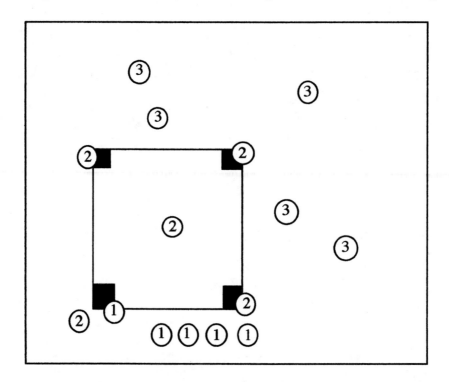

MODIFIED SLO-PITCH

SKILL OBJECTIVES: Most softball skills except base stealing and bunting

EQUIPMENT: Bases; gloves; catchers mask; bat; one softball

GAME SETUP: Divide the class into two equal teams with one team batting first and the other team in fielding positions. If a team has more than nine players, have "rovers" play in-between some of the regular positions.

HOW TO PLAY: This game is played exactly like regular softball with the following exceptions:
1) The pitcher must pitch a slow underhanded toss that rises no more than 10 feet from the ground to the batters.
2) The batter must take full swings at the pitch and can not bunt.
3) A batter hit by a pitch is not awarded a free base. Otherwise, strikes and balls are called as in regulation softball.
4) Baserunners can not "lead-off" (That is, he must not leave a base until a ball is pitched).
5) There is no stealing allowed by the baserunners.
6) A team bats until everyone has had a chance. Teams are to switch places at that time. Three outs result in the batting team clearing the bases of any baserunners.

SCORING: Same as in regular softball. The team with the highest number of runs at the end of a designated number of innings wins the game.

MAT KICKBALL

SKILL OBJECTIVES: Throwing; catching; kicking; baserunning.

EQUIPMENT: Three tumbling mats; one home base; one foam soccer ball.

GAME SETUP: This game is best played inside the gymnasium; however, it can be played outside as well. Set up the bases much like a softball field with a home base and tumbling mats for first, second, and third bases.

   Divide the class into two equal teams with one team assigned to kick first and the other team in fielding positions.

HOW TO PLAY: This game is played very much like Kickball (see game) with the following exceptions:
1) Baserunners have to circle the bases twice to score.
2) There can be an unlimited number of baserunners at one time on first, second, and third bases (not home base). Because of this, there are no force-outs in this game. Baserunners do not have to run on a kicked ball at any time during the game. The large tumbling mats provide adequate space for the baserunners to stand.
3) There is no leading-off or stealing by the baserunners. Baserunners must stay on the base until the kicker has kicked the ball.
4) There are three ways to get a kicker or baserunner out. They include: catching a fly ball; tagging the baserunner with the ball while not on a base; and a foul kicked by the kicker.
5) Each kicker is allowed only one pitch. A foul kick results in an out.
6) Teams switch places after 5 outs have been committed by the kicking team.

SCORING: One point is awarded for each baserunner that successfully circles the bases twice.

CHAPTER ELEVEN

GOLF

GOLF GAME PROGRESSION GUIDE

GAME	GRADE LEVELS			
	K-2	3-4	5-6	7-8
Beanbag Golf	X	X	X	
Soccer Golf		X	X	X
Frisbee Golf		X	X	X
Miniature Croquet Golf		X	X	X
Mini Golf		X	X	X

BEANBAG GOLF

SKILL OBJECTIVES: Beanbag throwing; golf scorekeeping; golf etiquette

EQUIPMENT: One beanbag for each player; nine hula hoops; nine numbered cones; scoresheets

GAME SETUP: Set up the golf course by placing the hula hoops about 10-20 feet apart in a scattered formation. Put a cone, with a number (1-9) attached to it, in the middle of each hula hoop. Depending on the number of players, set up multiple courses.
　　Place 3-6 players at each course.

HOW TO PLAY: Here's a great game for that rainy day, although it can be played outside as well. It's an especially good activity for teaching golf scoring to your younger students. The skill of underhand throwing, used in so many other sports, is also utilized in this activity.
　　To begin, a player underhand throws a beanbag toward the first hole (the hula hoop), trying to land it inside the hoop. In order, the other players do the same. Continue until all the players have "holed-out." The player with the lowest score (that is, the fewest throws attempted to land the beanbag into the hula hoop) throws first for the next hole.
　　Players should use a scoresheet or keep a running tab of the number of throws it takes to land the beanbag into each hole.

SCORING: Challenge the players to complete the course in the fewest number of "strokes".

SOCCER GOLF

SKILL OBJECTIVES: Kicking; golf scorekeeping; golf etiquette

EQUIPMENT: One soccer ball per player; nine hula hoops; nine cones with flag markers; scoresheets

GAME SETUP: Set up the golf course by placing the hula hoops about 40-60 feet apart in a scattered formation. Put a cone, with a flag marker, in the middle of each hula hoop. Depending on the number of players, set up multiple courses. Assign 3-5 players to a course.

HOW TO PLAY: Basically, this game is regular golf with the exception that kicking is used. This would be an appropriate soccer lead-up game as well.

To begin, a player kicks a soccer ball toward the first hole (the hula hoop), trying to have it land inside the hoop. In order, the rest of the players do the same. Continue until all the players have "holed-out." The player with the lowest score (that is, the fewest shots attempted to get the ball into the hula hoop) kicks first for the next hole.

Players should use a scorecard or keep a running tab of the number of shots to place the soccer ball into each of the holes.

SCORING: Challenge the players to achieve the lowest score possible.

FRISBEE GOLF

SKILL OBJECTIVES: Frisbee throwing; golf scorekeeping; golf etiquette

EQUIPMENT: One frisbee for each player; nine hula hoops; nine cones with flag markers; scoresheets

GAME SETUP: Set up the golf course by placing the hula hoops about 40-60 feet apart in a scattered formation. Put a cone, with a flag marker, in the middle of each hula hoop. Depending on the number of players, set up multiple courses.
   Assign 2-5 players to a course.

HOW TO PLAY: This game is much like regular golf with the exception that frisbees are used to make holes.
   To begin, a player throws a frisbee toward the first hole (the hula hoop), trying to get it to land inside the hoop. In order, the rest of the players do the same. Continue until all the players have "holed-out." The player with the lowest score (that is, the fewest throws attempted to place the frisbee inside the hula hoop) is allowed to throw first for the next hole.
   Players should use scorecards as a way of keeping track of the number of throws it takes for the frisbee to land inside each hole.

SCORING: Challenge each player to complete the course in the fewest number of "strokes".

CROQUET GOLF

SKILL OBJECTIVES: Croquet striking; golf scorekeeping; golf etiquette

EQUIPMENT: Nine wickets (numbered with tape); one mallet and ball for each player. Scoresheets, if available, would be handy in keeping track of individual scores.

GAME SETUP: Set up a nine hole golf course with the wickets as a substitute for the holes (about 10-20' apart). Tape a number (1-9) on each wicket. Depending on the number of students, set up multiple courses. Place 2-4 players at each course.

HOW TO PLAY: As the name of this game implies, this is actually minature golf played with a croquet set. The wickets are used as the holes and croquet striking is used to hit the ball.

To begin, a player tees off by hitting the croquet ball toward the first hole (the wicket). In order, the rest of the players do the same. Continue until all the players have "holed-out." The player with the lowest score (that is, the fewest shots attempted to hit the ball through the wicket) will tee-off first for the next hole.

Players should use scoresheets to keep track of their score.

SCORING: Challenge the players to complete the course in the fewest number of "strokes".

MINI GOLF

SKILL OBJECTIVES: Short golf shots; golf scorekeeping; golf etiquette

EQUIPMENT: A golf club and ball for each player; nine hula hoops; nine cones with a numbered flag inside each one. Scoresheets would be useful.

GAME SETUP: Set up the golf course by placing the hula hoops about 20-40 feet apart in a scattered formation. Put a cone, with a numbered flag inside, in the middle of each hula hoop. Depending on the number of students, set up multiple courses.
   Assign 2-4 players to a course.

HOW TO PLAY: Before playing, all students should have already been taught how to swing a golf club, as well as knowledge of safety precautions. This game is especially suitable for beginners because of the large holes (the hula hoops) and short distances.
   To begin, a player hits the golf ball toward the first hole (the hula hoop), trying to get it to land inside the hoop. In order, the rest of the players do the same. Continue until all the players have "holed-out." The player with the lowest score (that is, the fewest shots attempted to land the ball into the hula hoop) gets to tee-off first for the next hole.
   Players should use scoresheets or keep a running tab on the number of shots taken to land the golf ball into each of the hula hoops.

SCORING: The player with the lowest overall score wins.

CHAPTER TWELVE

BOWLING

BOWLING GAME PROGRESSION GUIDE

GAME	GRADE LEVELS			
	K-2	3-4	5-6	7-8
Beanbag Bowling	X	X		
Aerobic Bowling	X	X	X	X
Soccer Bowling		X	X	X
Frisbee Bowling		X	X	X

BEANBAG BOWLING

SKILL OBJECTIVE: Underhanded rolling for accuracy

EQUIPMENT: One beanbag for each player; 3-5 plastic bowling pins

GAME SETUP: Set up a bowling lane with the pins placed about 20 feet away from a throwing line. The bowling pins need to be in a tight triangular shape. Set up multiple lanes with 2-3 students assigned to each "bowling lane."

HOW TO PLAY: This game is very popular with the younger students because of the closeness of the pins and the familiarity of the beanbag.

Only three or five pins are required for this game but you can add additional pins if available.

Players are to use an underhanded throwing motion with the beanbag sliding toward the pins. The object is to hit as many as possible. Players should rotate between throwing and setting up the pins for the next bowler.

Regular bowling rules can apply however, the younger players will appreciate the simplicity of adding up the number of pins knocked down as a way of keeping score.

SCORING: If keeping score, the winner in each group is the player who knocks down the highest number of pins. Challenge the players to knock over as many pins possible.

AEROBIC BOWLING

SKILL OBJECTIVE: The underhanded bowling roll

EQUIPMENT: One bowling pin and ball (an indoor bowling ball or playground ball) for each set of partners

GAME SETUP: Have the students pair up. Place a bowling pin about 20-30 feet away from where the roller stands. One partner starts as the bowler while the other stands by the pin.

HOW TO PLAY: This is a great activity for developing bowling skills. It also has the added attraction of providing plenty of movement for the students.

As stated above, one partner begins as a bowler and the other stands ready to set up the pin after it has been hit. When the bowler releases his ball, he starts running toward the pin, ready to switch places with his partner. The partner who set the pin up now becomes the bowler. Play continues in this fashion throughout the game.

Encourage the players to run the entire time.

SCORING: Encourage each player to hit the highest number of pins possible.

SOCCER BOWLING

SKILL OBJECTIVES: Kicking; bowling scorekeeping

EQUIPMENT: Ten bowling pins and one soccer ball per bowling alley. Scoresheets would be useful for keeping individual scores (available at many bowling alleys).

GAME SETUP: Set up a bowling lane that's about 3-4 feet wide and 30-35 feet long. The 10 pins are set in a triangular shape. Depending on the number of students, set up multiple lanes. Assign 2-4 players to each lane.

HOW TO PLAY: This is regulation bowling with the exception that the balls are kicked instead of rolled by hand. Because of the kicking, this can also be an excellent lead-up game to soccer.

   After instructing the players about bowling scoring, hand out a scoresheet to each player. Players are responsible for keeping their score. Each bowler is allowed two balls per frame, for ten frames, for each game. Three games are a match. Players are to rotate between bowling and setting pins up.

SCORING: Regular bowling scoring.

FRISBEE BOWLING

SKILL OBJECTIVES: Frisbee throwing; bowling scorekeeping

EQUIPMENT: Ten bowling pins and one frisbee for each bowling lane; scoresheets for all players (available at many bowling alleys)

GAME SETUP: Set up a bowling lane that is about 3-4 feet wide and 30-40 feet long. The 10 pins need to be set in a bowling formation. Depending on the number of students, make multiple lanes. Place 2-4 students to a lane.

HOW TO PLAY: This is regulation bowling with the exception that the pins are hit with a thrown frisbee instead of with a ball.
   Each bowler gets two throws per frame, for ten frames, for each game. Three games are a match. Players are to rotate between "bowling" and setting up pins.

SCORING: Regular bowling scoring.

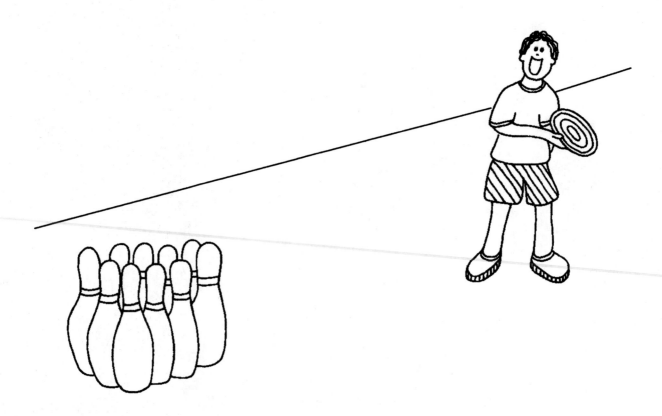

CHAPTER THIRTEEN

MISCELLANEOUS SPORTS

MISCELLANEOUS SPORTS GAME PROGRESSION GUIDE

GAME	GRADE LEVELS			
	K-2	3-4	5-6	7-8
Beanbag Horseshoes	X	X	X	X
Modified Bocce	X	X	X	X
Bocce Croquet		X	X	X
Croquet Billards		X	X	X
Cricketball		X	X	X
No Tackle Rugby		X	X	X
One Chance Rugby		X	X	X
Deck Tennis		X	X	X
Outside Billards		X	X	X
Mini-Team Handball		X	X	X

BEANBAG HORSESHOES

SKILL OBJECTIVE: Underhand throwing

EQUIPMENT: Two hula hoops; four beanbags

GAME SETUP: Group 2-4 players to a game (multiple games can be played simultaneously). Place two hula hoops about 15-30 feet apart.

HOW TO PLAY: The is the traditional game of Horseshoes, except that beanbags and hula hoops are used in place of the metal equipment. The hula hoops and beanbags offer a safer and more success-oriented setting for children.

   When throwing, players must stay behind the hoops. Each player is allowed two throws at a time. The objective is to land the beanbag inside the hula hoop for a "ringer."

SCORING: A beanbag that lands in the center of the hoop (a "ringer") counts as 3 points. A beanbag that ends up being the closest to a hoop (without a ringer being made) counts as 1 point. The first player (or team) to score 15 points wins the contest.

MODIFIED BOCCE

SKILL OBJECTIVES: Rolling; throwing for accuracy

EQUIPMENT: Two balls for each player; one center ball for each playing area. The center ball must be a different type of ball than the type the players are rolling (croquet balls, softballs, baseballs, etc).

GAME SETUP: Each playing area needs to be about 4 x 15 feet in size. Mark off a throwing line with the center ball placed about 12-15 feet away. Assign 2-5 players to each game. Depending on the number of students, set up multiple game areas.

HOW TO PLAY: This is a modified version of the very old but still popular Italian game of bocce. Bocce is considered the front-runner to the modern game of bowling.

For the most part, bocce rules apply. Players throw or roll their balls (each player has two) attempting to hit or land closest to the center ball. If only one hit is scored, that player is considered the winner. A player that throws the ball on the fly and hits the center ball would win over a hit made on the bounce. In the event where more than one player hit the center ball, they would continue throwing until a winner is declared. If no center ball hits are made, the winner is the one with a ball closest to it.

It's permissive for the thrower to knock an opponent's ball away or another one of his balls closer to the center ball.

SCORING: The player that hits the center ball with his ball (without the other players doing so), or comes closest to the center ball, is declared the winner.

BOCCE CROQUET

SKILL OBJECTIVE: Rolling a ball for accuracy

EQUIPMENT: Equal number of balls balls per person; croquet wickets; one croquet stake; chalk or tape to outline the throwing circle

GAME SETUP: Set up multiple game areas as needed. The bowling circle has a radius of about 3 feet. Set up a row of wickets about 20-40 feet away, with a stake at the end.
   Assign 3-6 players to each game. Players are to decide a rolling order.

HOW TO PLAY: This game utilizes the skill of rolling (used in bocce) with the equipment used in croquet. It's also a fun game to play when there's not enough mallets to go around for all your students.
  The objective is to roll a ball from the bowling circle through all 3 wickets to hit the stake.
  Before playing, each of the players should have an equal number of balls (3 or 4 is ideal). Players are to roll one ball at a time and are to stay in a predetermined rolling order.
  A player has to roll from inside the circle. As stated, the objective is to roll accurately enough so that the ball makes it through all three wickets hitting the stake.
  Remove each previously rolled ball so that each player has a clear field to the stake.
  Stepping outside the circle while bowling results in a violation. The ball does not count and the player loses his chance.

SCORING: A stake hit is 5 points. A ball that goes through all three wickets but does not hit the stake, is worth 3 points. A ball going through two wickets earns 2 points, and a ball getting through one wicket earns 1 point. Game winner is first player to reach 15 points.

CROQUET BILLIARDS

SKILL OBJECTIVE: Croquet striking

EQUIPMENT: Three croquet balls and one mallet for each game; caulk or cones for marking boundary lines

GAME SETUP: With caulk or cones, set up a 10 x 25 foot field (pool table shaped) as shown in the illustration. Depending on the number of students, design several game areas.

Assign groups of 3-5 players at each contest area. Players should determine a playing order before starting the contest.

HOW TO PLAY: This is a good game alternative when regular croquet begins to pall. The kids will enjoy the idea of playing a billard-type game in an outside setting.

Only three balls are used in this game. One is used as a cue ball and two are used as billiard balls. The objective is to hit the cue ball so that it strikes both billiard balls before stopping. This is called a "billiard", and counts as a point. A player keeps taking turns until he misses a billiard.

SCORING: One point for each "billiard." First player to get 15 points wins.

CRICKETBALL

SKILL OBJECTIVES: Throwing; catching; batting

EQUIPMENT: One base; one cone; one bat; one softball (or whiffle ball) for each game

GAME SETUP: Place a cone and base in a straight line about 30-40 feet apart. Depending on the number of students you have, design several game areas.

Assign 4 players to each game. There will be a pitcher, batter, catcher, and fielder.

HOW TO PLAY: This game contains skill elements of both softball and cricket.

The pitcher begins by throwing the ball toward the cone, which the batter is standing in front of and off to the side. If the pitcher hits the cone, it counts as a strike. If the batter hits the ball, he runs to the far base and back, without stopping, before the catcher is thrown the ball. If successful, the batter scores a run for himself. If unsuccessful, the batter is out. Unlike softball, tagging and catching fly hits do not count as outs.

After each out or run, players are to rotate positions. The batter becomes the fielder; the fielder moves up to pitcher; the pitcher goes to catcher; and the catcher becomes the new batter.

SCORING: A batter gets a point for himself if he successfully hits the ball and runs to the base and back before the catcher has possession of the ball. The player with the highest number of points at the end of the game wins.

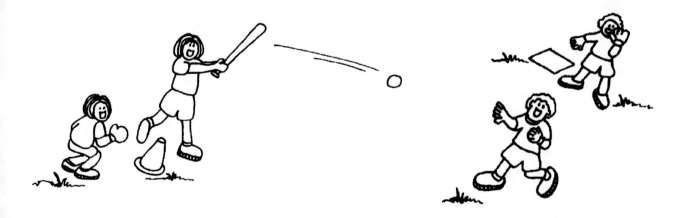

NO TACKLE RUGBY

SKILL OBJECTIVES: All basic rugby skills except tackling

EQUIPMENT: One rugby ball (or football) per game

GAME SETUP: A playing area of 30 yards by 50 yards would be ideal. Form two teams of 6-9 players each. Designate a team to kick off first from about mid-field. Team members should decide positions such as backs (2-3), safety (1), and linemen (3-6).

HOW TO PLAY: The game begins with a kickoff. The ball can be either punted or kicked. The player receiving the kickoff advances the ball toward the opponents' goal line until touched with two hands (a tackle).

Each team has three downs to advance the ball 10 yards. If successful, a team is allowed another set of three downs. If not, or if the ball is intercepted, the other team takes over the ball at that spot.

Players are to line up with the linemen's shoulders in contact. The center begins play by kicking the ball to any member in his backfield. Backs are to run forward or lateral to advance the ball. No forward passing is allowed.

Defensive players try to touch (with both hands) any player with the ball. This counts as a tackle and the play ends at that spot. Teams are to position themselves for the next play.

Fouls are called for unsportsmanlike conduct, defensive holding, being offsides before the ball is centered, and for passing the ball forward. Fouls result in the ball being moved up, or set back, 5 yards.

SCORING: One point is scored for a team when it has successfully touched the ball down inside the opponents' goal area.

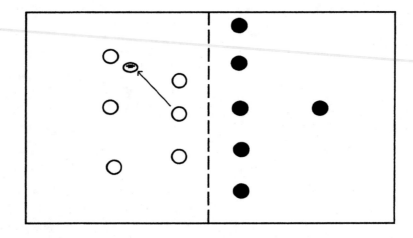

ONE CHANCE RUGBY

SKILL OBJECTIVES: All rugby skills except tackling

EQUIPMENT: One rugby ball (or football) for each game

GAME SETUP: A playing area of 30 yards by 60 yards would be ideal. Form two equal teams of 4-9 players each. Half of the players start as linemen and half as backs. Designate one team to start the game on offense with the ball on the midfield spot.

HOW TO PLAY: This is a fun lead-up game to a sport that has long been a favorite in Europe, Australia, etc., and is rapidly gaining popularity in this country among our youth. This activity involves no tackling, making it safe to use in a school setting.

The game begins with one team in possession of the ball at midfield with one chance to score. The linemen (half of the players on offense) line up with shoulders in contact. The center hikes the ball to one of the backs who then run forward or lateral to advance the ball down the field. Backs are also allowed to pass the ball backwards to a teammate at anytime. The play is over when a defensive player touches an offensive player with possession of the ball, an offensive player runs out of bounds with the ball, a backward pass is dropped, a pass is intercepted by a defensive player, or if an illegal forward pass is attempted. When a play ends, the opposing team gets the ball at the spot where the ball is downed, and now have their one down to score.

TEACHING SUGGESTION: Linemen should not be encouraged to be overly aggressive in their blocking. Reinforce that hands and elbows be held close to the chest at all times. Basically, linemen want to act as human shields, resulting in the defensive players having to run around them.

DECK TENNIS

SKILL OBJECTIVES: All deck tennis skills

EQUIPMENT: One volleyball net; deck tennis ring

GAME SETUP: Form teams of 6-9 players. Players are to be positioned as in volleyball. Add an additional court for larger-sized classes.

HOW TO PLAY: Deck tennis is often used as a lead-up game to volleyball and as an activity to develop throwing/catching skills. However, it is actually a regular sport by itself and is also a nice change-of-pace game from the other net-type games that kids play.
   The game begins with a serve (an underhand throw or frisbee style throw) from the back service line over the net. The player receiving the serve must catch the ring and throw it back across the net with the same hand he caught it with. If the ring is dropped or touches the floor, it becomes either a point or sideout (depending on which team was serving). All throws must be done in either an underhanded or frisbee style motion. Players with possession of the ring can not walk with it.
   Volleyball rules are used for rotating servers, scoring, etc.

SCORING: As in volleyball, the first team to 15 points wins, provided they have a 2 point advantage.

OUTSIDE BILLIARDS

SKILL OBJECTIVES: Kicking for accuracy; billiards strategy

EQUIPMENT: Fifteen smaller-sized soccer balls; one playground ball; twelve cones. Chalk or tape will be needed to mark off the boundary lines.

GAME SETUP: Set up a 15 x 25 foot billiard shaped playing area as shown in the illustration. Put two cones (about 2 feet apart) down at each of the six billiard "pockets." Depending on the size of your class, set up multiple playing areas.

The ten soccer balls need to be put in a tight, triangular shaped formation at one end of the field, with the cue ball (playground ball) at the other end.

Assign 2 teams of 2 players (4 players total) to each of the billiard fields.

HOW TO PLAY: This is a great activity for practicing kicking skills and introducing some of the basic elements of billiards. The additional exercise that comes from playing outside adds to the fun of this game.

Players are to take turns kicking the cue ball (the playground ball) at the billiard balls (the soccer balls), trying to knock one of them into a pocket (through the cones). Any player that successfully makes a shot is allowed to keep kicking until he misses.

SCORING: The player with the highest number of balls hit through the pockets wins the contest.

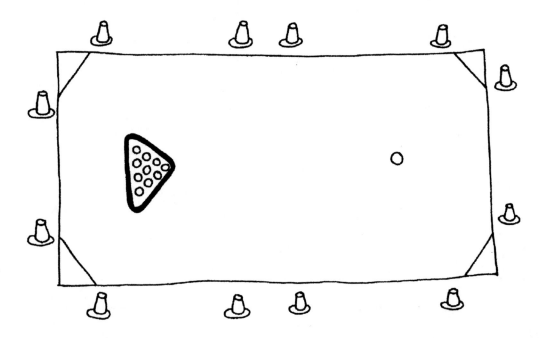

MINI-TEAM HANDBALL

SKILL OBJECTIVES: Throwing; catching; defending

EQUIPMENT: Pinnies; one foam-type ball; six cones; six beanbags

GAME SETUP: This game can be played either outside or in the gym. The size of the playing area can vary depending on the age of the students. For most students, a field size of 30 x 60 feet will work fine. Set up three cones, with beanbags on top, along the backside of each goal.

Form two teams of 4-6 players each. Each team has one player at the goalie position.

HOW TO PLAY: This is a lead-up game that is very successful for developing the skills and strategies related to the international game of team handball.

The objective is to score by throwing the ball at the opponents' goal past the goalie, and knocking off one of the beanbags on the cones.

The game begins with a jump ball in the middle of the court. Players can only pass to a teammate or throw at the goal. No running or steps are allowed once a player has possession of the ball. A player only has up to 5 seconds to pass or shoot. A violation results in the other team taking possession of the ball at that spot.

Defensive players are to guard an offensive player much as in basketball. No touching of an offensive player is allowed, nor can a defensive player knock the ball out of another player's hands.

After a score, the team scored against takes possession of the ball and the game continues.

SCORING: One point is scored for each goal.

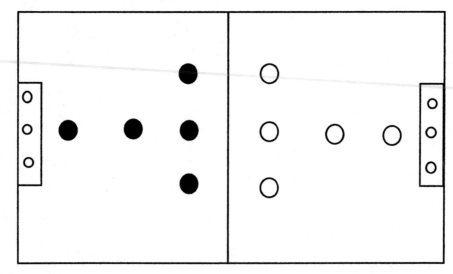

INDEX

ALPHABETICAL LISTING OF GAMES

A-B-C Relay, 132
Add 'Em Up, 193
Aerobic Bowling, 212
Aerobic Football Kicking, 40
Air Raid, 133
Around The Horn, 182
Around The World, 93

Backstop Soccer, 62
Bamboozle 'Em Football, 23
Baserunning Relay, 181
Basketball Golf, 98
Basketball Pirates, 88
Basket Bordenball, 104
Battle Ball, 29
Beanbag Bowling, 211
Beanbag Golf, 203
Beanbag Horseshoes, 217
Big Ball Volleyball, 136
Birdie Keep It Up, 145
Birdie Relay, 143
Bocce Croquet, 219
Boom It Over, 38
Bull In The Ring, 90

Capture The Footballs, 33
Catch 22, 127
Circle Pepper, 72
Circle Race, 110
Circle Soccer, 56
Clean The Court, 154
Crab Soccer, 49
Cricketball, 221
Croquet Billiards, 220
Croquet Golf, 206
Crosse Softball, 81

Deck Tennis, 224
Diamond Run-a-Round, 76
Dribble Freeze Tag, 53

End Zone, 35
End Zone Basketball, 99
End Zone Lacrosse, 78

Fake 'Em Out, 37

Field Goal Contest, 39
Five Catches, 25
Five Passes, 96
Flicker Football, 43
Floor Ping Pong, 157
Fly Back, 74
Flying Birdies, 138
Four Ball Shootout, 57
Football 100, 34
Four Downs, 41
Four Square Volleyball, 140
Four Team Soccer, 67
49 'er Football, 36
Frisbee Bowling, 214
Frisbee Golf, 205

Goalies Galore, 119
Gotcha !, 89
Ground Attack, 116
Grounder Ball, 184

Half-Court Basketball, 101
Heading Relay Races, 61
Hike 'N Catch, 26
Hike & Pass, 30
Hit The Board, 137
Hockey Keep-Away, 114
Hockey Pirates, 109
Hockey Steal, 111
Home Run, 196
Home Run Football, 31
H-O-R-S-E, 92
Horse Tennis, 160
Hot Tators, 183
Hula Hoop Discus Throw, 171
Hula Hoop Long Jumping, 170

In A Pickle, 185

Keep Away, 75
Keep It Up, 129
Kickball, 186
Kick-Off Attack, 32
King of the Dribblers, 91
Knock 'Em Down, 27
Knock Out, 100

Lacrosse Tennis, 80
Line Hockey, 115
Line Soccer, 59
Long Base, 194
Loose 'N' Limber Tag, 166
Lotsa Pucks, 118

Mass Badminton, 149
Mass Soccer, 47
Mat Kickball, 200
Miniature Croquet Golf, 206
Mini Golf, 207
Mini-Team Handball, 226
Modified Bocce, 218
Modified Hockey, 123
Modified Shot Put, 172
Modified Slo-Pitch, 199
Modified Soccer, 68

Newcomb, 128
No-Ball Football, 21
No Net Badminton, 146
No-Outs Kickball, 189
No-Outs Softball, 197
No Racket Tennis, 158
No Rules Basketball, 87
No Rules Tennis, 156
No Rules Volleyball, 130
No Tackle Rugby, 222
No-Team Softball, 195

One Chance Football, 42
One Chance Softball, 192
One Chance Rugby, 223
Outside Billiards, 225

Pass Ball, 97
Pass Relay, 73
Pickleball, 162
Pin-Ball Soccer, 55
Points Galore, 135
Pony Express, 168
Position Hockey, 122
Possession, 77
Punt and Pass Relay, 24
Punt Attack, 28
Pyramid Passing, 112

Rotation Soccer, 66

Royal Lacrosse, 83
Runners & Gunners, 95
Run 'N' Gun, 44
Run 'N' Weave, 113

Sack The Quarterback, 22
Scoop Crosse, 79
Scores Galore, 63
Serve 'Em Over, 134
Shooting Goals, 117
Shuttle 'Minton, 147
Sideline Basketball, 106
Sideline Hockey, 121
Sideline Lacrosse, 82
Sideline Soccer, 60
Sideline Volleyball, 128
Slugger Ball, 190
Soccer Bowling, 213
Soccer Croquet, 65
Soccer Golf, 204
Soccer Maniacs, 50
Soccer Pirates, 54
Soccer Red Light-Green Light, 48
Soccer Steal The Bacon, 57
Soccer Tunnel Tag, 51
Sprint Tag, 167
Stretch Tag, 165

Team Cross Country, 169
Team Olympics, 173
Tee-Ball, 188
Tennis Dribble Relay, 153
Tennis Keep Away, 159
Tennis Knockout, 155
Tennis 'Round The World, 161
The Soccer Bull, 52
Throw & Go, 71
Throw & Go, 187
Three And Over, 139
Three On Three, 102
3-On-3 Hockey, 120
3-On-3 Mini-Soccer, 58
Three Team Softball, 198
Throw & Run Softball, 191
Triple Play, 103
Twenty-One, 94

V-O-L-L-E-Y, 131
Volleyminton, 148

Each day you have the golden opportunity to create a laboratory of life in your gymnasium – to give your students life changing knowledge and experiences. Relish the possibilities.

Guy Bailey

ABOUT THE AUTHOR

Guy Bailey, MEd, is an elementary physical education specialist for the Evergreen School District in Vancouver, Washington. Guy has over twenty years of experience teaching K-8 grade physical education. During this time, he has also coached numerous youth sports and intramural activities. He received his Bachelor's degree from Central Washington University and his Master's degree from Portland State University.

In addition to this book, Guy has also authored *The Ultimate Playground & Recess Game Book*, a unique resource of over 170 playground and recess activities for K-8 grade students.

Guy's professional goal is to equip each of his students with a love of movement and the basic skills needed to participate in an active lifestyle now and as adults. He believes that for long-lasting skill development to take place, physical education needs to consist of success-oriented learning experiences that literally leave students craving more. This book reflects Guy's philosophy of using skill-based activities that are fun, exciting, and meaningful.

In his spare time, Guy enjoys jogging, reading, writing, weightlifting, hiking, and fishing the beautiful Columbia River near his home town of Camas, Washington. He also has a passion for college athletics and is a frequent visitor to PAC-10 stadiums and gymnasiums throughout the Pacific Northwest.

Guy is also an active member of the *American Alliance Of Health, Physical Education, Recreation and Dance,* and is frequently requested to speak at educational conferences around the country.

EDUCATORS PRESS
INFORMATION & BOOK REQUEST

To order additional copies of *The Ultimate Sport Lead-Up Game Book*, please contact your favorite bookstore or catalog company. You can also order directly from the publisher. Call (360) 834-3049 or write to the publisher's address listed below to order by check. For faster processing and/or credit card purchases please call toll-free:

1-800-431-1579

This book, as well as *The Ultimate Playground & Recess Game Book*, are available at quantity discounts. Contact the publisher for more information.

Educators Press
5333 NW Jackson St.
Camas, WA 98607
(360) 834-3049